If you *only* knew...

If you *only* knew...

Unmasking The Hidden Pain
In Your Church

O. SONNY ACHO

Scripture quotations are taken from the *New American Standard Bible*®, Copyright © The Lockman Foundation 1960, 1962, 1963, 1968, 1971, 1972, 1973, 1975, 1977, 1995. Used by permission.

Library of Congress Cataloging-in-Publication Data

Acho, O. Sonny, 1951-
    If you only knew : unmasking the hidden pain in your church/ O. Sonny Acho.
        p. cm.
    Includes bibliographical references.
    ISBN 0-8024-3305-7
    1. Church work. I. Title.

BV4400.A24 2003
253—dc21
                                        2003000879

1 3 5 7 9 10 8 6 4 2

Printed in the United States of America

To my wife, Christie, who is always understanding and patient while I fulfill seemingly endless commitments and responsibilities. Your unwavering support has been a blessing to me.

CONTENTS

ACKNOWLEDGMENTS

I would like to thank my children for their inquisitiveness. Their frequent questions about my completion date helped light a fire under me to complete this book!

My thanks to Rhonda Kimble, who, through her editing skills and creative insight, organized my thoughts and brought structure to each chapter.

Finally, I am grateful to the Fellowship Ministry staff at Oak Cliff Bible Fellowship and my private-practice staff for offering constant encouragement during this project. With their assistance, I was able to carve out precious time from a hectic schedule to sit down and write.

FOREWORD

Hospitals are a vital part of the well-being of any community. Their fundamental purpose is to address the problem of physical pain. These institutions are uniquely staffed and equipped to meet people who come to them with the resources necessary to address their pain.

Pain shows up at the door of hospitals in a multiplicity of ways. Some pain is minor, only needing mild medication. Other pain is deep and even life threatening, requiring emergency surgery. Wherever along the spectrum a patient's problem lies, the hospital is prepared to administer help. Its primary mission is to take the pain away.

The church was established by God to heal the spiritual pains of those who come for help. It has been uniquely gifted and equipped to address the many needs that come her way.

It's not enough for the church to function like a medical school, dispensing information about the nature of sickness and pain and the appropriate treatment. Rather, the church is to be the primary care center for the many struggles and pains of its members. Those who are spiritually sick due to their sin, the sins of others, or simply from the challenge of being in a sin-infested world need to know that God's hospital, the church, is the best place to go to find healing in an environment of love and acceptance. Unfortunately many Christians and churches are ill equipped to effectively address the pain of its members.

The church is not a hospice, a place where people go to die. Hospitals, unlike hospices, are designed to promote and restore life. Thus, the person bringing his pain to the church must, of necessity, want to get better. It is not the job of the church to simply make people comfortable in their pain, but to diagnose its cause and administer the appropriate spiritual cure to relieve it so they can lead fully victorious Christian lives.

In this book, my friend and co-laborer Sonny Acho, like a hospital's chief of staff, identifies some of the major spiritual ailments that show up at the doors of the church today. Like a good doctor, he goes beyond mere diagnosis to treatment, showing us how God wants us to address these ailments.

This fine work will sensitize you to a better understanding of your pain and the pain of those around you while at the same time helping to equip you to be a more effective spiritual physician who is able to treat others.

If You Only Knew will prepare individuals, leaders, and churches to be more effective in their God-given responsibility of being spiritual doctors under the direction of our Great Physician.

Dr. Tony Evans

INTRODUCTION

When I began working on this introduction, I was asked to list my credentials—what gave me the "authority" to write this book. *A reasonable task,* I thought. *I have a Ph.D. in counseling. I headed up a private practice for sixteen years. I've been married for twenty years, I've raised four children, and I've been preaching and ministering for almost thirty years.* But I quickly realized that my career and personal accomplishments would not necessarily prove my worthiness to write a book on unmasking hidden pain. Only my perspective and observations can do that.

In my career as a professional counselor and in my role within the church as associate pastor, God has blessed me with the ability to see various sides of particular situations. For example, I've seen gifted leaders and pastors who are eloquent speakers and amazing teachers of Scripture on Sunday. But Monday through Saturday they privately struggle with intimately personal issues including maintaining a successful marital relationship, control and leadership difficulties, sexual temptation, and maintaining integrity.

I've seen people enter church looking well put together on Sunday morning. They worship the Lord fully and wholeheartedly. You would imagine that their lives are in order and running smoothly. But some of these same people come into my private-practice office during the week to discuss problems with physical and sexual abuse, addiction, guilt, marital affairs, lack of trust, and major financial struggles. As a counselor, I always welcome those who are seeking to better their emotional and spiritual well-being. Yet there appears to be an unhealthy degree of secrecy involved in this healing process.

My church offers group counseling for a variety of issues such as grief, chemical addiction, and marital conflicts. As head of the counseling ministry, I am responsible for making the rounds to see how the support groups are faring. Imagine my surprise when I realized that most of the group sessions were empty or rarely attended!

I am barely able to squeeze into my calendar all the people who seek help privately (most of whom attend my church). While I would love to believe it is my personal counseling style that has people flocking to see me, I know better. People want to keep their struggles and issues secret, even within the Christian community. Why? Because the church has made them believe that their issues aren't welcome. Therefore, few people expose their battles, and if they do, they do it behind closed doors. They are dying on the inside in an effort to mask their pain with a happy face.

The reasons for this dichotomy vary. Some people believe Christians shouldn't have problems, especially not ones that may make other people uncomfortable, or make believers appear to be like the secular people from whom we are trying to distinguish ourselves. Others want to preserve the image of a fruitful church so desperately that they turn their backs on people who, if helped through their struggles, could be more fruitful than anyone can imagine.

I believe it is necessary to bring to light topics that have been in the dark long enough. Only by acknowledging, addressing, and offering solutions to these problems can people begin to open up and be honest about them.

It is my prayer that you will develop the courage to look beneath the surface of your own issues, and the issues of others, so that you may find comfort and healing. Through this process, you can experience fullness of life in Christ.

O. Sonny Acho, Ph.D.

PREFACE

People love to look good. Consider the care we take in putting ourselves together on Sunday mornings. We come into church with not one hair out of place, dressed in impeccable clothes. When we arrive, some of the members assess the way the others are attired with barely perceptible glances of disapproval.

Her dress should be a little longer.
His suit doesn't cover his expanding waistline like he thinks it does.
That man's belt and shoes aren't even the same color.
Why is she wearing linen slacks after Labor Day?

Conversely, stares of quiet admiration assess the luxury cars pulling into the church parking lot.

I wonder what she does for a living.
Look at the rims on those wheels—could they be any shinier?

If that were my car, there's no way I'd park it next to any of those others.

The couple in the Brooks Brothers suit and the Calvin Klein dress ascend the stairs leading to the balcony, where they sit beside the Armani suit and the Donna Karan ensemble. Everyone notices the person wearing the tattered clothing and feels pity for that "unfortunate" person.

We are often so focused on looking good on the outside that we do not even consider what's going on in the heart. We become masters of deception as we cover up our true condition. Because on the inside, most of us are filled with pain.

The two women seated next to each other in their designer clothing know nothing about each other's hurts. They exchange polite pleasantries during the worship service, but neither of them realizes that the other was barely able to emerge from the house that morning. One woman spent all night crying and arguing with her husband at the unexpected discovery of his extensive pornography collection. The other is hoping the service will be over quickly so she can rush to the drugstore for some bottled water and aspirin, having just come to terms with the fact that she is a functioning alcoholic. Neither of these ladies would think of talking to the other because they are too lost in their respective pain. They are afraid that if they took a chance and shared their stories, they would be alienated by some and judged by others. So they politely take their seats and hide their heartache.

We have all experienced pain in one way or another at various times. God never promised a pain-free life.

One of the sources of pain is sin. With the fall of man, sin crept into the world, and it has become a part of our everyday lives. All humans—even believers—are imperfect. Although we have died to sin, we are not totally free from it as long as we still live in our fallen bodies.

In Genesis chapter 4, when Cain found out that his sacrifice was not acceptable in God's eyes, he became angry and bitter toward God. God warned Cain about harboring sin in his heart. "Sin is crouching at the door; and its desire is for you" (verse 7). Sin was waiting for an opportunity to express itself in Cain's life. Cain should have listened to God and obeyed Him. Since he did not deal with his sin, Cain turned his anger on his brother Abel and killed him.

But not all pain is related to sinfulness. For example, the grief experienced when a death occurs is not caused by sin, but by the loss of a loved one. Other circumstances, such as medical problems, accidents, or crimes perpetrated against us, can be overwhelming. Since our behavior was not the cause of the pain, we don't have any idea how to deal with the devastating emotions involved.

Some of us have so much pain in our lives, we are unwilling to even talk about it. So we become bitter and resentful toward everyone, shutting ourselves off from any sort of meaningful relationship for fear that someone might uncover our pain. We assume we can deal with it without anyone's help. Since no one can really help us, we reason, we must suffer alone. And therefore, we slowly die . . . alone.

Most of us are experts at camouflaging our pain. We dress in our best clothes, primp our hair, and don a dazzling smile, but inside we are dying. When someone asks how we are doing, we automatically respond, "Great!"

Now, I am not saying that we should go around looking somber and solemn all the time and complain about every little disturbance. Ecclesiastes 3:1 says, "There is an appointed time for everything. And there is a time for every event under heaven." There is "a time to weep and a time to laugh" (verse 4). It would be as strange to mourn during a party as it would be to laugh at a funeral. We need to admit that pain is real and then deal with it in a timely fashion.

The Christian life is meant to be lived within a community. As part of a community, you risk being sinned against as well as sinning against someone. It can be tempting to keep a safe distance from others. But we cannot live in a community of believers and not get involved in one another's lives. Galatians 6:1–2 says, "Brethren, even if a man is caught in any trespass, you who are spiritual, restore such a one in a spirit of gentleness; each one looking to yourself, so that you too will not be tempted. Bear one another's burdens, and thereby fulfill the law of Christ."

The community of believers within a local church is a great tool for individual healing. Leaders should encourage members, via sermons and personal interaction, to care for one another. Every church needs an effective biblical counseling program that can walk a person through the Scriptures to find encouragement and hope.

Church leaders must be willing to get involved in the lives of the congregation. James 5:14 instructs the sick to "call for the elders of the church" and let them "pray over him." Verse 16 says, "Therefore, confess your sins to one another, and pray for one another so that you may be healed."

Today, the preaching of the Word has become so central in our churches that we can sometimes forget the people. Doctrine is essential. Without it we would not have a correct view of how we are to live. But if we stress the academic side of ministry and leave out the personal side, we have missed the boat.

Christ was constantly involved in the personal side of ministry. He took time to visit people in their homes. We should be willing to follow His example.

Preaching in the pulpit is not enough. Though it has its place, it does not fully address the issues with which people are attempting to cope. In Exodus 18:16, the people came to Moses with their individual and group issues. He had such a long line of people wanting him to spend time with them that he had to assign others to help him with the task.

Many people have been beaten up by the world and need to find hope and encouragement. The church is to be a haven for hurting people. The apostle Paul was willing to be "in labor" with the Galatian church until Christ was formed in them (Galations 4:19). If we are to reflect God's glory in our churches, we must be willing to get into people's lives and help them become more like Christ.

Are you willing to deal with the pain in your own life as well as the lives of the people around you? If so, read on.

1

If you *only* knew...
<u>My Guilt</u>

Physical pain is usually so uncomfortable that we must find relief from it. Sometimes relief is sought through visiting a physician and/or taking medications.

Guilt often feels just as bad as physical pain. It can result in emotions of restlessness, fear, panic, or worry. Feelings of guilt are often related to the shame of having sinned. Since Christians are expected to live up to a biblical standard of moral behavior, admitting that they have fallen short is a challenge for many. In an attempt to hide the sin, they may also hide the guilt that accompanies it. They attempt to ignore the pain of sin and guilt through denial, acting as if they simply don't exist.

Guilt is defined by *The American Heritage Dictionary*[1] as "the fact of being responsible for the commission of an offense." An alternate definition is "remorseful awareness at having done something wrong." But let's see what the Bible says about it.

James 2:10 reads, "For whoever keeps the whole law and yet

stumbles in one point, he has become guilty of all." In the New Testament, guilt is described as a conviction of sin. It arises when someone has broken God's holy and righteous standard. Therefore, we may *feel* guilty whether or not we truly *are*. Guilty feelings are not necessarily an indication that we have done wrong, nor is a lack of guilty feelings necessarily an indication that we have behaved correctly. James 2:10 doesn't say that the person who stumbles over one point and *feels* guilty is "guilty of all." It says that he who stumbles *has become* guilty of all, regardless of his emotional state.

SOURCES OF GUILT

Guilty feelings can be a necessary part of getting ourselves aligned with God's will and purpose for our lives. But sometimes guilt comes from a source other than God.

Unrealistic Expectations

As we are growing up, family members communicate, via expressed thoughts and actions, their expectations for us. In many cultures being the firstborn son carries extra responsibility. Parents expect their oldest boy to be successful in all he does and to care for his younger siblings. A first son may feel guilty if he doesn't provide for his brothers and sisters, even after they are adults and should be responsible for their own lives. If those siblings behave irresponsibly, the eldest son may be expected to bail them out or at least to feel guilty for not doing so.

Oldest siblings, regardless of gender, are typically expected to excel more than their brothers and sisters in school or in their careers, and they often have the greatest restrictions put upon them while growing up. Parents hold many hopes, dreams, and desires for their firstborn children.

Because of the pressure put on them to meet expectations, eldest children often grow up feeling guilty for not becoming everything their parents anticipated. In many instances the oldest in a family is the Rock of Gibraltar, while the youngest lives a life of carefree irresponsibility.

In many cultures wives must have hot meals ready for their families every day. They are also expected to give birth to as many offspring as the husband wants. If they fall short, they are chastised by their spouses.

These expectations create a major conflict when a person from one cultural background marries someone who has been raised in a different culture. For example, a modern woman may wonder how her husband can expect her to hold down a full-time job and still cook hot meals every day. "Why can't we go out to eat, order pizza, or bring home fast food once in a while?"

If an individual doesn't live up to what is expected of him, no matter how unrealistic those expectations may be, he is almost certain to feel guilty.

Inaccurate Biblical Teaching

Some people feel guilty if they miss a Sunday morning worship service or fail to pay their tithes regularly. Perhaps you worship in a legalistic church, or you have a spouse, pastor, fellow parishioners, or friends who consistently send the message that God is a mean, uncompassionate Father who is just waiting for you to mess up so He can condemn or punish you.

Too often we are programmed to believe that God's love is conditional. While Scripture is full of commands that God requires us to obey and descriptions of the consequences that are suffered when those commands are not followed, God's love is always present in the believer's life. Romans 5:8 says, "While we were yet sinners, Christ died for us."

I accepted Christ as a young man in 1970 and joined a church where watching TV, going to movies, and allowing women to wear makeup or nail polish were forbidden. I remember passing judgment on my mother whenever she put on makeup. I thought, *How can she be saved and live such a worldly lifestyle?* I tried many times to make her feel guilty based on what I thought. Years later, I had to ask my mom to forgive me for the way I judged her in my days of ignorance.

Even though I know it is legalistic, I still view many things through the filters of my upbringing. For example, I married someone who shares my disinterest in movie watching. If I had married someone who wanted to go the movies every weekend, we would have been in trouble.

One woman I counseled felt guilty because a Christian who claimed that God always spoke audibly to him prophesied to her regarding something he claimed the Lord wanted her to do. Maria was deceived into believing that the Lord has specially anointed "favorite children" to whom He gives messages so they can pass them on to the "less favorite" children. When she was unable to obey this person's message by giving the amount of money he said God wanted her to give, and by marrying the one God told him to instruct her to marry, Maria was burdened with guilt.

If you are a child of God and are living for Him, He will speak to you *directly* concerning issues that regard you. Other saints may confirm His instruction by their testimonies.

We see a good example of this in Genesis 24:10, when the servant of Abraham went to the city of Nahor to get a wife for his son Isaac. When he arrived at the home of Rebecca, her father and older brother said, "The matter comes from the Lord" (verse 50). The Spirit laid it on their hearts that Abraham's servant was sent from God, so they confirmed the message by their comments and by their lack of resistance.

If the message you receive is not confirmed by biblical teaching, you should wait, pray, and seek more clarity before proceeding with it. You don't need to be in a hurry to believe anything except the message of salvation.

Past Sin

Sin always carries strong feelings of guilt once it is recognized. If we were able to predict the extent to which we would experience guilty feelings after sinning, that would likely deter us from engaging in it so frequently. But often we forge ahead, oblivious of the price we will pay. Then, after we've sinned, our conscience convicts us of our unrighteousness, with the ultimate goal of repentance. Because a lot of us are ignorant to the work of the Holy Spirit in that area, we tend to use guilt to condemn rather than convict.

In my practice, I have counseled many people who have committed grievous sins. Often during counseling sessions it becomes clear that these people were well aware that they were courting danger before they made the choice to sin. After their decision wreaked havoc with their lives, they were burdened by guilt that disrupted their peace. Their conscience was attempting to convict them for the purpose of repentance, but instead, conviction turned into condemnation that lasted for years.

If you are holding on to guilt from your past sins, don't think that God is pleased. He is not interested in how you feel about your past sins, but only your action toward your present temptations.

Not long ago, I counseled Jackie, a forty-eight-year-old single professional who seemed to have it all together. She was beautiful, and she had a good job, a steady income, and an impressive house. At a conference near her home on the East Coast, she met Jeff, who lived on the West Coast. During dinner one night, they felt a strong attraction toward each other. Jackie and Jeff began a long-distance relationship, seeing each other as often as time and money would allow.

When Jeff starting telling Jackie how much he cared for her and that he wanted to spend the rest of his life with her, she thought it was too good to be true. The Holy Spirit hadn't confirmed that he was "the one" for her. However, since she had a deep fear of aging alone, Jackie made a rash decision instead of waiting and trusting God. That was her first sin. Then she began sleeping with him. They married a short time later, but after a few years, Jeff told Jackie he didn't love her anymore and he was filing for divorce.

For years after, Jackie was plagued with guilt for her sinful decisions with Jeff.

Sue, a single parent for five years, came into my office with guilt based on poor decisions she had made in the past. Sue was raising three children whose deadbeat dad was either unwilling or unable to financially provide for his children's necessities. Sue struggled with trying to be both mother and father to her children. Recognizing that she didn't have what it takes to raise three kids by herself, she started playing the "If Only" game:

> If only I had continued to put up with my husband's physical, emotional, and verbal abuse, the children would still have their father. We would have a house, and participate in more activities, and go on trips. Everything would be like it used to be.
>
> If only I had been a better wife and not been disrespectful to my husband, he would have given me the love and respect God commanded him to give.
>
> If only I had honored my mother and father and listened to their admonitions, I would have gone through premarital counseling to find out if God had truly ordained my marriage.
>
> If only I had stayed true to myself and God and kept my virtue, I wouldn't have had children out of wedlock and felt the need to "settle" just to make sure the kids had a father . . . any father.

The "If Only" game expresses a hope to change the past. But that's not possible. We can't get it back, so constantly reliving our poor choices will only frustrate and limit us. Healing begins when we consciously put the past behind us. We must press on with what we have now and deal with our problems as they currently exist.

I recommended to Sue that she hold a family council to discuss their situation. She needed to:

1. Confess her bad decisions to the children. Ask for their forgiveness, pray, and determine to move forward.
2. Remind the children that she is still their mother.
3. Focus on the blessings their family has.
4. Realize that their hope and trust are in the Lord, not in a dad.

In Nehemiah chapter 2, Nehemiah reported on the sad condition of the city of Jerusalem. It had originally been surrounded by walls and gates to protect it. But when those walls were burned and torn down, Nehemiah realized that security was at risk. He spent a brief time in confession of national sin and recognizing the spiritual poverty of the people. Then he devised a plan for reconstruction that utilized the human and material resources that were on hand or could be requisitioned.

There are four key elements in this story:

1. Nehemiah had to ask for some things.
2. He had to direct talented people.
3. He had to delegate tasks and create work assignments.
4. His actions were sourced in prayer and he was fully dependent on God.

Single parenting is a project that uses these same ideas:

1. You have to ask for some things.
2. The family unit should be organized and structured, balanced and fair.
3. Everyone in the family has a responsibility and should be designated tasks according to his or her individual talents.
4. The family is to be bathed in prayer, which teaches the children the value of and need for it. Prayer then becomes an indispensable part of their lives.

There is nothing we can do to change our past. Focusing on it only keeps us from looking to the future and seeking ways to do things differently. We can become stagnant, paralyzed by guilt.

The only action required to deal with past sin is to confess it to God and receive the forgiveness He has granted in Christ. If you have never accepted Jesus Christ as your Savior, that is the first step. First

John 1:9 states that when confession is made, Christ forgives. When we accept this precious gift from God, we can get beyond the pain in our past and move forward to new life in Him.

TYPES OF GUILT

Many people believe that guilty feelings are harmful to one's emotional well-being and, therefore, should be silenced. Others will tell you that guilty feelings are necessary to act properly and to be obedient to our Lord and Savior. So, are guilty feelings bad or good?

If feelings of guilt are not dealt with properly, they can cripple, hold hostage, and eventually destroy a believer. Guilty people may praise God, pray fervently, take diligent notes of the pastor's sermons, and hug their brothers and sisters in Christ. But inside they are torn apart about something they have done.

When someone requests prayer for her marriage, she may be feeling extreme guilt over something she did that jeopardized her relationship with her husband. Her guilt may even blind her to a possible solution to the problem. She prays, yet has no real expectation that God will forgive her. Or she begs for forgiveness because she feels like she should, but she has no real regret over what she did.

There are two types of guilt: unhealthy and healthy.

Unhealthy Guilt

Unhealthy guilt can be classified into three categories: silenced guilt, shouting guilt, and manipulative guilt. These are all based on our desire to take control of ourselves, things, or other people, which has the detrimental effect of removing God as Lord of our lives.

• *Silenced Guilt*

John F. MacArthur Jr. gives an interesting illustration in his book *The Vanishing Conscience: Drawing the Line in a No-Fault, Guilt-Free World.*[2]

In 1984 an Avianca Airlines jet crashed in Spain. Investigators studying the accident made an eerie discovery. The "black box" cockpit recorders revealed that several minutes before impact a shrill, computer-synthesized voice from the plane's automatic warning system told the crew repeatedly in English, "Pull up! Pull up!"

The pilot, evidently thinking the system was malfunctioning, snapped, "Shut up, Gringo!" and switched the system off. Minutes later the plane plowed into the side of a mountain. Everyone on board died.

If we ignore our "automatic warning system," we will "crash and burn." Silencing our conscience when we have done wrong is harmful. We put ourselves at risk of shutting down God's way of telling us we are in dangerous waters. God has given us guilt as a tool to allow us to grow and to alert us when we are not aligned with His will. If we don't heed the warning, sin will invade our lives and harm us, and possibly others.

I am currently counseling Gail, a thirty-five-year-old born-again believer who is a divorced mom raising her thirteen-year-old daughter, Amanda. Gail got involved with a thirty-eight-year-old man named Ronald. A few weeks after they began dating, she allowed him to move in. Soon after, her conscience went to work. She would go to the altar every Sunday to try to silence it, but it wouldn't stop bothering her.

Months later, she started noticing inappropriate closeness between Ronald and her daughter. One day Gail found out that she and Amanda were both pregnant by him. She had the pregnancies terminated, but is now dealing with a daughter who claims to be deeply in love with Ronald. He hates Gail for making Amanda abort the child. Amanda hates her mom and herself for the abortion.

When we refuse to obey our conscience, which God uses to warn us of sin and consequences, we have to face the pain and guilt of choosing to ignore it.

Silenced guilt manifests itself when people stubbornly refuse to give up sinful behavior. Because they feel they should be able to control their own destiny and make their own choices, they learn to shut off their conscience. A person who has silenced his guilt becomes skilled at ignoring the warning signs. He believes that his wants and needs are more important than God's will.

In Jonah 1:2, God commanded Jonah to preach to the Ninevites. He said, "Arise, go to Nineveh the great city and cry against it, for their wickedness has come up before Me."

Because of the history of the Israelites and the Assyrians, Jonah did not want to preach to the Ninevites. He feared they might repent and believe. Since Jonah realized that God is a "gracious and compassionate God" (4:2), he knew the Lord would forgive the Ninevites. Jonah may have thought that God didn't know what He was doing. After all, these were His enemies. They were wicked people. Jonah wanted them to get what they deserved.

Jonah may have rationalized his disobedience to God's command. *Why, there just happens to be a ship docked right here waiting to go to Tarshish,* he may have thought. *What perfect timing!* It seems that every time God gives us a command, there are a million opportunities to distract us from His will.

Jonah decided to go to Tarshish, which was in the exact opposite direction of Nineveh. But his rebellion landed him in trouble.

After the ship set sail for Tarshish, a great storm arose. According to Jonah 1:4, the storm was sent (literally "hurled") by God. Now, sailors were accustomed to storms, but this time they were afraid (verse 5), which indicates that this storm was exceptional. In fact, it was so powerful the ship was about to break.

Yet all during this massive storm, Jonah slept! He was so calloused that his sin did not affect him in the slightest. No guilty conscience kept him awake, even under such convicting circumstances.

I suspect Jonah slept because he was trying to avoid the voice of the Lord. The devil would like to convince us that if we ignore God's instruction, His voice will eventually go away.

The captain of the ship awakened Jonah and asked, "How is it that you are sleeping?" (verse 6). He commanded Jonah to get up and call on his God, for everyone else had been crying out to their

gods in hope that one would rescue them. Jonah knew that his bla-
tant disobedience was the cause of the life-threatening storm.

First Timothy 4:2 says that people can be "seared in their own
conscience." Titus 1:15 says, "To the pure, all things are pure; but
to those that are defiled and unbelieving, nothing is pure, but both
their mind and their conscience are defiled." You may feel the pangs
of guilt temporarily, but eventually become so used to them that they
no longer bother you. You have been "hardened by the deceitfulness
of sin" (Hebrews 3:13).

People go about their daily routines oblivious to how their actions impact others and how they may be displeasing God. They
do what feels right to them instead of comparing their behavior to
God's standard.

This type of guilt can affect your business, personal, and family relationships. If you don't deal with it, it can result in physical
and/or emotional problems. Constantly ignoring it will break fellowship with God. The only way to resolve the problem is to address
your transgression and ask sincerely for forgiveness.

• *Shouting Guilt*

Some people berate themselves to the point of ineffectiveness.
They have played their transgression over and over in their minds.
They believe they have passed the point of no return with regard
to forgiveness from the Lord. "You don't understand!" they exclaim.
"I've done something so bad that it will take a while for God to tru-
ly forgive me."

A woman named Sandy came into my office desperate for help
with suicidal thoughts. After several sessions I learned that she had
had seven abortions and felt that God had given up on her. Sandy
believed the first sin was bad, but forgivable. Yet as the number of
sins increased, the possibility for forgiveness decreased.

I told Sandy that God could forgive her for any sin, and any number of sins. All sin is equal in the sight of God, even though the
consequences of sin may be different. Though Sandy was guilty for

her sins, God had forgiven her. All she had to do was receive what already had been given: forgiveness.

Shouting guilt is rooted in a need to control. It develops when people decide to police themselves and the severity of their actions. Instead of believing God's Word—which tells us that if we ask for forgiveness and repent, He will forgive us our sins—those who hear the shouts of guilt use their own worldly standards to assess how they should be treated. This can lead to self-pity, depression, and suicidal thoughts.

People who victimize themselves to shouting guilt typically suffer from depression and inactivity. They are so bogged down with thoughts of their own worthlessness and inadequacy, they fail to see their strength in Christ, and their thought processes and actions reflect this limited view.

• *Manipulative Guilt*

Some people use guilt to manipulate others·when they don't live up to expectations.

Zach's mother never disciplined him as a child. She allowed him to run the streets and drink with his friends at an early age while she was busy with her prostitution business. As a young boy, Zach learned how to manipulate people to get what he wanted. He had even refused his mother's boyfriend access to the house until he paid Zach five dollars.

Zach's mother died when he was eleven years old, and he decided he had enough skills to survive on his own. Forty years later, with many legal problems including time in prison, Zach showed up in my office with his third wife, Courtney, who wanted to leave him because he was a master manipulator.

Courtney's chief complaint was that when she wanted to go out, Zach always asked where she was going and how long she would be gone. If she said, "Three hours," Zach would say, "You don't need to be gone that long." He often threatened, "If you leave me, I might get drunk and kill myself." He manipulated her through guilt.

In counseling, Courtney grew strong and started refusing to be manipulated. She learned to say, "I'm going to be gone for three hours, and if you choose to, you can blow your head off. However, I refuse to feel guilty and responsible for your behavior." As Courtney remained steadfast in her decision to not be responsible for Zach's choices, he eventually realized that his manipulative tactics no longer worked with her and he stopped the idle threats.

Since Zach opted not to face his own issues, he began to act out in other ways. But Courtney had regained a sense of control in her life, and his actions no longer devastated her.

Young couples, after dating for some time, often run into a roadblock because the man pressures the woman for a sexual relationship. They both know that becoming physically intimate would be an affront to God. But the young man insists that having sex will somehow prove her love for him.

An employer may offer favors to certain employees with the understanding that they will participate in unethical activities.

Even pastors sometimes manipulate their parishioners into tithing out of guilt instead of the grateful and loving attitude described in 2 Corinthians 9:7.

Control is at the root of this behavior. People become preoccupied with their need for others to adhere to their expectations. The silent message is, "If you do what I want, I will love you; if you don't, I will make you feel so bad that you will see how doing things my way is better."

The desire to control others leaves God out of the picture. It is not our responsibility to push people into following our agenda; it is God's responsibility to steer them toward His. Only He is sovereign enough to require obedience. With a loving and serving attitude, we are to encourage people to follow His plan, even if it does not align with what we would like to see happen.

Has someone coerced you into doing something that went against God's will because he was more interested in advancing his own goals? When you recognized what he was up to, how did it make you feel? How did you react when you realized that you had compromised yourself and the Word of God to accommodate this selfish person?

Manipulators destroy relationships by eroding trust. The person who has been manipulated feels angry, insulted, and mistrustful. He no longer knows what to expect from that person. The manipulator's ability to fellowship with God is also hindered.

Healthy Guilt

Robert S. McGee, author of *The Search for Significance,*[3] makes an important distinction by calling the healthy kind of guilt "conviction." He writes, "Guilt brings depression and despair, but conviction enables us to realize the beauty of God's forgiveness and to experience His love and power." Conviction is a positive agent that God uses for our sanctification.

If you are a believer, you possess the Spirit of God. When the Spirit is offended, conviction occurs as an alarm that something is wrong. Our fellowship with God, and usually with others, has been broken.

Automobiles are equipped with two kinds of warning systems. The first is a measuring device called a gauge. It measures the performance of the systems. When it begins to read out of the acceptable operating range, the car is in trouble.

The driver must do two things. First he must *read the gauges*. If he doesn't, he'll never know there is a problem. Second, he must *fix the problem*. If he fails to do this, the gauges serve no purpose.

The second kind of warning system is a light that comes on in the instrument panel. Once, in the days before cars were equipped with these warning lights, the automotive engineers of a particular car manufacturer received a complaint about an engine failure in one of their cars. An investigation revealed that there was no oil in the engine when it failed. The gauges were all found to be in good working condition. So the engineers concluded that the driver had ignored the gauges.

Now, the manufacturer of the car didn't want to lose the customer, even though the problem was the driver's fault. So the engineers were instructed to come up with a system that would alert the driver in a stronger way that would be more difficult to ignore.

The engineers designed a red light that would blink continuously until the problem was fixed. Only an idiot, they said, would ignore flashing red lights on a car that cost so much money! The manufacturer agreed, and the warning lights became a standard feature. To this day, they are called "idiot lights."

The Word of God serves as a gauge with which to measure and evaluate our conduct. When we ignore the instructions and statutes of the Word (or worse, when we don't read it at all), the "idiot light" called our conscience sends the alarm that we are seriously in need of a repair called confession before further damage in our relationship with God takes place.

Within the conscience of a Christian, guilt is a convicting mechanism that alerts us that we have:

- made a sinful choice;
- given home to a sinful attitude;
- sustained sinful thoughts;
- spoken sinful words;
- neglected our spiritual responsibilities.

We must repent of our sins. This involves several components:

- **Confess.** Admit your wrongdoing. Don't make excuses. Just agree with God that you have done wrong.
- **Apologize**. Begin with God. If your offense includes others, apologize to them as well. Acknowledge that you may have injured a relationship that is important to you.
- **Ask.** Seek forgiveness and a restored relationship with the person you have offended.
- **Commit.** Determine not to repeat the offense.

First John 1:9 defines the pattern for restoration between ourselves and God, and serves as the example for people to use with each other. We can forgive others for *anything* on the basis of those sins for which God has forgiven us. This is a conscious choice we make.

God binds Himself to His Word. Do we bind ourselves to ours? Consider what would happen if God forgave us only on the basis of how we forgive others. Aren't we blessed that He forgives on the basis of His shed blood and the promise of His Word? If we recognize and understand that blessing, it will change how we deal with the offenses of others.

Conviction is designed to help us grow. Without it, it would be difficult for us to recognize our wrongdoings and seek ways to right them. When I am in the wrong, I usually experience a lack of peace in my spirit until I correct my transgression, apologize to those I have offended, and go to God in repentance. Only when I take those steps do I experience a closer walk with God.

Some Christians argue that guilt only applies to unbelievers since they have denied Jesus as their Savior. But conviction is an experience that believers in Christ share. It is important for Christians to realize that when they sin and feel guilty, they have not lost their salvation. Sin removes us from fellowship, not from sonship. Restoring fellowship is possible through confession of the sin.

Healthy guilt, or conviction, always leads to repentance. Second Corinthians 7:10 says, "For the sorrow that is according to the will of God produces a repentance without regret, leading to salvation, but the sorrow of the world produces death."

Repentance does not mean merely feeling sorry. It is an admission of guilt followed by a turning away from sin and toward God. When you truly repent and turn to God, He will change your heart.

The Bible says Peter denied Christ three times and felt guilty when he realized that fellowship was broken. He repented, was forgiven, and moved back into fellowship. But Judas betrayed Jesus, felt guilty, and hung himself because he wasn't really of God. Two individuals felt the same thing; one repented, and the other chose destruction.

The result of conviction must be restoration. God doesn't want us to focus on our inadequacies. He never said we should remain fixed on our sins. He instructs us to confess our sins and deal with them appropriately, but not to meditate on them. We must let conviction drive us to the foot of the Cross so Christ can fill what is lacking in our lives.

We repent, not because we think we will somehow earn "extra credit" in God's eyes, but because we want to glorify God in our bodies (1 Corinthians 6:20).

OVERCOMING GUILT

How can we get beyond guilt to lead a productive life? Following are four actions we can take.

Keep a Clean Conscience

People are usually far more worried about the effects that dealing with sin will have on their reputation than on the effects that not dealing with sin will have on their relationship with the Lord. But if we persist in keeping sin hidden, we will never have a clean conscience.

In Acts 23:1 Paul said, "Brethren, I have lived my life with a perfectly good conscience before God up to this day." Does that mean Paul never sinned? No. Paul was human, just like we are. In this verse, he stated that he maintained a clean slate by confessing his sin and striving to live under the control of the Holy Spirit.

Know the Difference Between Healthy and Unhealthy Guilt

We must avoid the extremes of wallowing in pity and becoming hardened by the deceitfulness of sin. Finding a happy medium between the two should be our goal.

Suppose someone says to you, "You are worthless!" Either you believe it and live the lie, or you measure the accusation against your belief system. The correct way to deal with false guilt is to strengthen our knowledge of who we are in Christ.

What does God say about your worth? First Peter 2:9 says, "You are a chosen race, a royal priesthood, a holy nation, a people for

God's own possession, that you may proclaim the excellencies of Him who has called you out of darkness into His marvelous light."

Now, let's say you are feeling guilty because of the way you treated your spouse before you left for work this morning. And let's suppose that you really did treat him unkindly. Allow conviction to drive you to repent and straighten things out with your spouse. If you say, "I know God forgives me," and do nothing to right the transgression, you leave your mate hurting from the wounds you inflicted.

We must nourish our conscience by feeding it the Word of God. The only way we can know if we are in God's will is to study His Word. God's Word is a filter that keeps impurities from defiling our minds and hearts. For this reason, we must take "every thought captive to the obedience of Christ" (2 Corinthians 10:5).

Acknowledge Your Forgiveness

Robert Jeffress, in his book entitled *Guilt-Free Living*,[4] says, "For the last two thousand years mankind has been trying to hang a sign on the cross that says, 'Necessary . . . But Not Enough.' " Even after we have repented of our sin, we may feel a need to do something more. We think we need to earn God's forgiveness. Know that your sins are forgiven on the basis of Christ's sacrifice. If it were any other way, Christ would not have had to die.

John the Baptist warned his followers that they should bear "fruits in keeping with repentance" (Luke 3:8). But we should not confuse the fruit with the root. The root of forgiveness is the Cross. No more, no less. Christ's death is completely sufficient to forgive any sin. True repentance will always lead to a corresponding change in behavior. Since forgiveness is based on Christ's death, the fruit is simply evidence of what has already taken place.

Focus on Christ, Not Your Guilt

After we have evaluated our guilt and discovered that it is conviction, we must let it do its work in us. Then we must move on. Even though we may not be able to completely forget our past sins, we are to live as if they are dead. Christ has slain them by His death on the cross. In Philippians 3:13–14 Paul says, "Brethren, I do not regard myself as having laid hold of it yet; but one thing I do: forgetting what lies behind and reaching forward to what lies ahead, I press on toward the goal for the prize of the upward call of God in Christ Jesus."

Summary Points

✓ Guilty feelings are not necessarily an indicator that we have done something wrong. Conversely, the lack of guilty feelings is not necessarily an indicator that we are operating within God's will.

✓ Guilt originates from many sources and circumstances. We must pay attention to what is causing our feelings of guilt.

✓ There are two types of guilt:

Unhealthy guilt, which can be silenced, shouting, or manipulative. This guilt is destructive to our relationships with others and interrupts our fellowship with our Creator.

Healthy guilt, which is the loving conviction of the Holy Spirit. The purpose of this voice is to encourage us to repent, allow God to forgive us, and move on.

✓ We need to pay close attention to those around us so we can be aware when they are trying to make us feel unnecessarily guilty.

✓ We must shift our focus from our experiences to the Lord so we can glorify Him through our activities here on earth.

QUESTIONS TO PONDER

✓ How do I deal with guilt? Do I . . . ignore it? Constantly berate myself about whatever I did to feel guilty? Deal with it by allowing it to produce repentance?

✓ Am I attempting to control certain areas of my life that should be controlled by God?

✓ Am I glorifying God in my actions? Are my thoughts always on Him?

✓ Have I tried to get other people to conform to my idea of what I think they should do or be? Am I willing to separate people from my expectations of them?

2

If you *only* knew...
MY BITTERNESS

We usually imagine Christ as a gentle-spirited man who was profoundly patient and merciful. We think He was so perfect, He never became angry. But that is not an accurate depiction of our Lord. He became extremely angered at sin.

Some Christians have the mistaken impression that in order to project a Christlike image, we must always wear a smile and never get upset. Even when they are feeling angry at someone or something, these people utter a hearty "Praise the Lord!" and try to suppress the bitterness. They believe they would be betraying God if they admitted they were hurt.

Many people in the church today are in pain because they are holding on to bitterness. They believe it will go away with time if they ignore it. But eventually, bitterness will always make itself known.

Bitterness rears its ugly head when church staff members refuse to say a word to one another except at mandatory meetings because someone offended someone else, and the offended person refuses to address the offender with the goal of resolving the issue.

The principles of biblical confrontation are found in Galatians 6:1: "If anyone is caught in any trespass, you who are spiritual, restore such a one in a spirit of gentleness." Church members are not to gossip with other members or export their bitterness throughout cliques within the organization.

It is difficult to see how bitterness has pervaded the Christian environment because church people cover up the true state of their hearts.

Men and women often have difficulty forgiving their ex-spouses for offenses committed years ago. Some wives refuse to allow their ex-husbands access to the children because they still harbor bitterness. They want their children, parents, and siblings to have the same unforgiving attitude they do.

WHAT IS FORGIVENESS?

Some people think forgiveness means to simply "let go" and not be angry anymore. Others define it as forgetting the past and moving on. To me, it is choosing to not hurt your offender for hurting you, to not retaliate or punish someone for an offense against you.

Bitterness is a human reaction to an offense. By practicing it, we think we are hurting the one who has hurt us. We fail to realize that by being unforgiving, we hurt more than the one we are trying to hurt. The Greek word for *forgiveness* means "to release, pardon, or to let go." We forgive by letting go of our hurt and anger and treating the offender as if no sin has been committed.

To forgive doesn't mean to forget. Christ remembers all of our iniquities, yet forgives us as if we had never sinned.

The Gift of Forgiveness

All of us have experienced the joy of receiving a gift. The ones that bring the most joy are those that meet some specific need in our lives. The Bible tells us in John 3:16 that "God so loved the world, that He gave His only begotten Son, that whoever believes in Him shall not perish, but have eternal life." By giving us this precious gift, God met our greatest need: divine forgiveness.

God pardoned man from the penalty of sin. If you have not received this gift, you are missing out on a great deal. You can't enjoy life the way it is meant to be enjoyed without receiving the forgiveness from sin that only comes from God.

Forgiveness is also the greatest gift you can give to others and yourself.

Distinguishing Forgiveness from Reconciliation

Reconciliation means to "normalize" the relationship with the person you need to forgive. You may think that in order to forgive, you must resume a relationship with the person who hurt you. If you are not ready to do this, you may hold on to bitterness. But reconciliation and forgiveness are not the same. Reconciliation should only occur when the offender confesses, apologizes, and repents. Forgiving is your responsibility. But reconciliation requires some action from the offender.

A parent who abused a child may not be able or willing to apologize, repent, or pay any penalty for their sin. So reconciliation with that parent is not possible. But the person who was abused still needs to forgive the abuse. Not doing so prevents the wound from healing.

EXAMINING FORGIVENESS

Matthew 18:21–35 suggests that because we have been forgiven by Christ, we ought to forgive those who sin against us.

The forgiveness described in this text is human, not divine. Peter's question was, "How often shall my brother sin against me and I forgive him?" Peter's "brother" had committed a wrongful act against him enough times to get on Peter's last nerve. He wanted permission to strike back at those who were past their threshold of sin. Jesus told Peter he was not to strike back at all.

There is no limitation to forgiveness.

Two major points are established in verse 21. The first is that people are going to sin against you. It doesn't matter how nice you are or how lovable your personality. It won't matter where you've come from or where you're going. Something will happen that will require you to be forgiving.

The second thing is that forgiveness is something we all have the capacity to do. Peter didn't say, "How can I forgive my brother?" He asked how often he should forgive. Jesus' answer was "up to seventy times seven."

Jesus was not giving Peter a license to knock the brother out after the 490th sin. He was saying, "Peter, you have the capacity to forgive at all times."

Some of us have already determined how much we are willing to take from others. We are quick to demonstrate forgiveness the first one or two times we're wounded. But after that, we're at the end of our rope. But at this point we need to remember the tolerance God demonstrated toward us when we stood desperately in need of His forgiveness. Not only in reference to our salvation, but to the forgiveness He grants us daily for the wrongful acts we commit toward Him. Suppose, after our offenses toward God added up to "seventy times seven," He stopped forgiving us?

REASONS TO FORGIVE

We can easily come up with legitimate-sounding reasons to not forgive someone. But forgiveness has nothing to do with settling accounts.

When a bank loans someone money, and the person is unable to repay it, sometimes the bank will cancel the loan agreement. This not only benefits the borrower. Banks sometimes cancel debts because they want to reconcile their ledgers. Financial institutions have to account for the money they loaned out. Their ledgers must balance when they stand before the IRS.

We often think that by forgiving someone, we are doing them a favor. In reality, we're doing ourselves a favor as well. One day we are going to have to stand before the Lord. The divine auditor will examine our ledgers to determine our roles in heaven. Forgiveness not only benefits the one in need of forgiveness; it also helps settle the accounts of the offended one.

WHAT FORGIVENESS LOOKS LIKE

Starting in verse 23 of Matthew 18 Jesus told a parable that illustrates what forgiveness should—and shouldn't—look like.

Verse 24 says, "When he had begun to settle [his accounts] . . ." Forgiveness is a process that takes time. The process begins with two individuals coming together. "One who owed him ten thousand talents was brought to him." The king and the slave met in person. This is not to say that if getting together is impossible, forgiveness shouldn't take place. However, whenever possible, the offender should try to confess and apologize face-to-face.

The slave deserved to be sold, along with his wife, children, and all of his possessions so repayment could be made. But the king didn't give the slave what he deserved; he chose to show compassion (verses 25–27). Forgiveness is never based upon justice. It demonstrates mercy toward the one who has committed the transgression. I'm glad God doesn't give us what we deserve. If He did, we would need to close the doors of our churches, because none of us deserves to be in His house.

Verse 26 tells us the slave asked for mercy. In verse 27 it was granted. "And the lord of that slave felt compassion and released him and forgave him the debt."

WHAT FORGIVENESS IS NOT

Many believe that forgiveness is simply accepting someone's apology. But it is much more than that. Verse 28 says that the slave who experienced mercy from his lord sought out a fellow slave who owed him a hundred denarii. When the fellow slave asked that he demonstrate mercy toward him, the forgiven slave choked his peer and demanded his money.

In Luke 15:11–32, the prodigal son deserved to be forbidden from returning home. He should have been left out in the fields after he wasted his inheritance. His brother wanted to see the prodigal son get all he deserved. But the father was compassionate.

One reason it was hard for the brother to forgive was that he had unrealistic expectations. He thought everyone should live up to God's holy standard, just as he had. When others behave differently from what we expect, we judge, condemn, and become embittered.

We can't pick and choose which behaviors we'll forgive. God doesn't classify or categorize sin. Psalm 86:5 says, "For You, Lord, are good, and ready to forgive, and abundant in lovingkindness to all who call upon You."

Since we've been forgiven, we ought to be forgiving, because God can use our pain and frustration to help others.

Forgiving Is Not Always Easy

It is easier to talk about forgiveness than to practice it. As you read this chapter, your mind may flash to certain family members, coworkers, old friends, and acquaintances who have offended you. You need to take a serious look at whether you have thoroughly forgiven them as God has commanded.

It's not easy forgiving a husband who has lied, or a child who continually disobeys, or a wife who strayed, or a boss who promoted everybody except you, or a parent who abused you, or a brother who constantly harassed you.

Forgiveness may cost us our pride. It may even cost us some money. But no matter how hard it may be, it will never be as costly for us as it was to God. The greatest act of forgiveness was when God forgave us. God had to give His only begotten Son.

HOW TO FORGIVE

Ask the Holy Spirit to tell you if there is someone in your life you need to forgive. Contemplate whom your debtors might be.

There may be someone in your life of whom you need to ask forgiveness.

You have the opportunity to show compassion to that individual. You can settle an account with another as well as with yourself. Do it today.

Unresolved issues will hinder your prayers. In Matthew 5: 23–24, Jesus said, "If you are presenting your offering at the altar, and there remember that your brother has something against you, leave your offering there before the altar and go; first be reconciled to your brother, and then come and present your offering."

Forgiving Yourself

Jessica and Patrick's marriage of three years was in great danger when Jessica made an appointment to see me for counseling. Patrick was in the military, and while he was fulfilling an overseas assignment, Jessica fell in love with the next-door neighbor. She got pregnant and decided to have an abortion. Patrick returned home, and the marriage seemed great for a year. But Jessica struggled with her sin. That led to sexual problems, which they brought to me as the apparent issue.

In one of my sessions with Jessica, she revealed her affair and the abortion. She said, "I know God has forgiven me. I'm sure that when I tell my husband he will forgive me, too, but I'm having a problem forgiving myself."

Self-forgiveness may be the biggest problem counselors deal with today. The Bible clearly speaks of horizontal forgiveness (giving and receiving forgiveness from one another) and vertical forgiveness (God forgiving an individual), but there aren't any passages that specifically address self-forgiveness. However, this concept is covered under the umbrella of guilt, conviction, and God's grace. (See chapter 1 on this topic.)

After several sessions with Jessica, it became obvious that she did not understand God's forgiving grace. She was, in essence, saying, "I have done too horrible a thing to be forgiven."

Though she believed 1 John 1:9, which says, "If we confess our sins, He is faithful and righteous to forgive us our sins and to cleanse us from all unrighteousness," Jessica didn't truly believe that a holy

God would forgive a sinner like her.

She continued receiving counseling and meditated on Ephesians 1:4–5, which states, "Just as He chose us in Him before the foundation of the world, that we would be holy and blameless before Him. In love He predestined us to adoption as sons through Jesus Christ to Himself."

Eventually, the idea finally sank in that God had chosen her to be His child and forgiven her long before she ever came into being. When Jessica finally understood that God forgave her, she was able to forgive herself.

SUMMARY POINTS

✓ The act of forgiving is the greatest gift God gave to us through His Son, Jesus Christ. It is also one of the greatest gifts we can give to others and to ourselves.

✓ Forgiveness and reconciliation are not the same. We are commanded to forgive, that is, to pardon offenders for the sins they have committed against us. We are only to reconcile with offenders when they have confessed, apologized, and repented.

✓ We benefit ourselves when we forgive because we remove an internal burden and "balance our ledger" with God.

✓ Forgiveness involves compassion on behalf of the person who was wronged. It requires the strength to avoid exacting revenge or penalizing the violator. This is not always an easy process.

✓ The Holy Spirit can direct us to seek and offer forgiveness.

QUESTIONS TO PONDER

✓ Is there anyone I need to forgive for some issue, whether petty or significant, recent or old?

✓ Do I fully understand the extent of God's forgiving mercy? Do I appreciate the wonderful gift He gave me: His Son?

✓ Do I have some predetermined level or quantity of offense beyond which I refuse to forgive?

✓ Is there someone I need to approach or contact to ask for forgiveness?

3

If you *only* knew...
MY MARITAL CONFLICTS

During courtship, most people have no idea how difficult living with each other is going to be. They fail to realize that the majority of married couples go through struggles. Just as human bodies occasionally require healing, there are times when marriages need to be repaired. And healing rarely takes place in a vacuum.

Marriage is a fragile entity that needs constant loving care. But too often people get impatient and look for a quick fix. They want to avoid pain at all costs.

HIDING THE CONFLICTS

Married couples often feel pressured to present a perfect union before the church. In today's world, image is everything. Partners are reluctant to discuss their problems with the pastor or even fellow members of the congregation. So they present a false image of a happy marriage while they privately struggle to stay together.

Not long ago, a successful businessman named Mel came to

me, having been court ordered to seek anger management counseling. Within minutes he began to cry. "I'm almost fifty years old.
I have never in my life fought a man, much less a woman. I can't
imagine how I could have beat my wife."

Mel said he had been married for twenty years, and over time
he became increasingly frustrated at his wife's frequent oversights to
pay their bills on time. After one more conversation about the same
old topic, he snapped. He beat his wife mercilessly.

When the ambulance arrived to take his wife to the hospital, police arrested Mel. As he was being handcuffed, he moaned, "Honey,
I'm sorry. I don't know what got into me."

Through our sessions Mel began to get in touch with his years
of unhappiness, which he masked in making money and buying luxury items, including changing cars every nine months. He had never said anything to his wife about this because he wanted to preserve
his "Mr. Nice Guy," under-control image. He suppressed his feelings,
until that fight over the water bill.

Many of us sweep our feelings under the rug. When we can no
longer hide them, we explode with anger or escape into drugs, alcohol, work, or sexual affairs.

GOD'S ORIGINAL PLAN

Most of us think we have what it takes to pull off a successful
marriage. We sometimes fail to realize that marriage is a God-created
institution that serves a God-designed purpose. In Ephesians 5:32,
the relationship between a husband and wife is called a mystery, one
that should reflect the relationship between Christ and the church.

God designed marriage for the purpose of glorifying Him. He
meant it to be a wonderful and enjoyable thing. But, like everything else God created, marriage has guidelines and principles we
must follow in order to realize its full benefit.

Years ago, when my children were younger, I often purchased
toys that required many frustrating hours to put together. Sometimes
my children would hand me the manual, but I thought, *I don't need
that. I've got a Ph.D. This can't be difficult.* But I didn't manufacture the

toys. The makers knew something I didn't, which is why they took the time to print instructions.

God's Word is the instruction manual for marriage. Many marriages struggle because one or both spouses refuse to follow the Maker's instructions.

WHAT IS TRUE LOVE?

Our society has done an outstanding job of convincing people that romantic love is the best love. We see images of couples gazing into each other's eyes, young lovers professing their undying devotion, a man dropping to one knee asking for his beloved's hand in marriage. Advertisers use the hope of romantic love to coax us into buying everything from engagement rings to deodorant soap. Romantic love sells. It grabs our attention and keeps it. It sounds promising, and we often think it will solve most, if not all, of our problems.

But what about the love God describes as the best kind we can give to another person? It is much deeper than the fluffy, cute, warm-fuzzy, romantic love we see in the media. This kind of love can extend to a mate, a child, a parent, a friend, even an enemy. First Corinthians 13:4–7 says, "Love is patient, love is kind and is not jealous; love does not brag and is not arrogant, does not act unbecomingly; it does not seek its own, is not provoked, does not take into account a wrong suffered, does not rejoice in unrighteousness, but rejoices with the truth; bears all things, believes all things, hopes all things, endures all things."

How many of us have experienced this kind of love? Have you been courageous enough to give a love like this?

I love my children as much on their worst days as on their best. I love my family unconditionally and completely. This kind of love is a choice, not a feeling. When I make the decision daily to love them, through God's grace, my heart follows my decision. I am compassionate, respectful, uplifting, encouraging, and connecting toward my wife. I make sacrifices so my children can grow spiritually, emotionally, intellectually, and physically.

I have made a decision to love my family irrespective of what they do to "earn" it. You can never really earn the gift of being loved. Neither can we children of God earn our way into His heart through our behavior.

How have I come to love so deeply? I have a perfect model and demonstration of love in Jesus Christ. It is overwhelming to think about the depth of God's love for us. But we are to model that kind of love on this earth. When we really connect with godly love, we feel compelled to extend that love to others.

When you invest in the stock market, you assess a company to determine whether or not its business practices are sound. You take a look at market conditions. You deposit your money and hope for the best. If you have made some insightful observations, you will likely make more money, over time, than what you put into the stock. But you cannot be assured that you will receive a return on your investment.

The same holds true for marriage. Galatians 6:7 explains that "whatever a man sows, this he will also reap." If you want peace in your home, sow a spirit of peacefulness. If you want gentleness from your mate, sow gentleness into your mate. Looking for honesty? Be honest. Give what you want to get, and watch for the bountiful harvest.

Now, if you invest in your mate, you will not necessarily get back *from your mate* what you put into him. God promises that you will reap the seeds you sowed. However, don't limit Him by anticipating the source of the harvest. In some cases, if you sow a compassionate heart into your spouse, you may receive compassion from another source—perhaps a parent, trusted friend, or even a stranger.

An investment also requires sacrifice. A person should not expect to retire a millionaire if he is only willing to invest three dollars per paycheck. That small investment, even over a long period of time, will probably not amount to much. The same holds true for marriage.

Investing requires patience. In the past decade, the booming economy's prosperous stock market enabled people to receive double the return on their investment in a few short years. But how long did that last? When the recession hit, people lost tens of thousands of dollars overnight.

Wise investors stick it out through shaky times because they know they will get more money in the long run. Marriages are no different. If a wife has some emotional baggage from previous relationships, the husband should be patient with her and take the time to help her through those issues. The reward will be a wife who is so grateful for her husband's patience that she will do everything she can for him.

Consistent investing pays off. Ecclesiastes 11:6 says, "Sow your seed in the morning and do not be idle in the evening, for you do not know whether morning or evening sowing will succeed, or whether both of them alike will be good."

Infrequent "grand gestures" mean nothing if you are not taking care of your loved ones in small, everyday ways. Surprising your wife with a weekend getaway at a tropical vacation spot once a year is nice, but if you have not been looking after her the other 364 days a year, the gesture will not mean much. It will be perceived as insincere and "too little too late."

Don't get discouraged if you don't see results right away. Sometimes it may be necessary to give more than you planned in order to get something back. Other times it won't require much of an investment at all.

Tuning in to your mate's needs isn't really hard. Husbands, pay attention to what your wife wears and compliment her if it's something you like. Chances are she will make a point of wearing that outfit again, to please you and to receive more flattering comments.

Sometimes people are so afraid that their investment of love won't pay off, they don't bother trying. The stakes—pain, heartbreak, or embarrassment—seem too high.

If giving love has had a bad outcome in the past, or if you believe there is only so much love to go around, you may be stingy with your love. You will wonder what people are going to take from you, how they will take advantage of you, or what a fool you will look like if you choose to love. Instead of demonstrating patience, you will be short-tempered because you are on the defensive. Instead of being understanding and compassionate, you will be critical and judgmental.

A person who doesn't understand how much he is loved in Christ will more than likely be unable to love others in a godly way. His love will be limited and will go only as far as his closed heart lets him.

The inability to give love is a sign of low self-esteem. If I am confident in who I am in Christ, I have forgiven myself for my transgressions because He has forgiven me. I understand there is no finite amount of love to give and receive, so I am willing to extend a loving heart toward others.

It is important that spouses understand how God's love impacts them. Only through that understanding will they be able to give love to each other.

ROLES WITHIN MARRIAGE

People often think their contributions to the marriage should be equal, that marriage is fifty/fifty. They try to give their 50 percent and hope their spouse will bring hers. That is a purely societal view.

Genesis 1 and 2 state more than six times that God created man and placed him in the garden to cultivate and keep it. The picture in that passage is one of a gardener whose responsibility is to take care of the grounds. He knows when it needs to be watered, cut, and fertilized. These verses indicate that God called the man to the specific roles of manager and leader.

In Genesis 2 God said it was not good for Adam to be alone, at which point He provided a helpmate for him. Much has been written about the word *helpmate*. It means simply "one who is brought alongside to support and assist." Right from the creation of the marriage institution, God gave the man a job, a responsibility, and an instruction. He put the burden of responsibility for the home on Adam, not Eve.

Woman was originally created to assist the man. Women were

never meant to bear the burden of responsibility for the home and family. When couples go against God's order of marriage, they usually suffer consequences, including lack of peace.

The chief complaint of most women I counsel is that their husbands don't fulfill their leadership roles. Most of the men respond, "She won't let me!"

COMMUNICATION

In the early 1900s, less than two out of one thousand marriages in the United States ended in divorce or annulment.[1] The US Census Bureau now estimates that 50 percent of all first marriages could end in divorce.[2] One major contributor to divorce is a lack of communication.

Effective communication is essential for any successful relationship. Pilots cannot take off and land successfully without clear communication between them and the air traffic control staff. The American military cannot successfully fight terrorism without an advanced communication mechanism that allows them to predict the enemy's next move. Likewise, couples cannot enjoy a fruitful relationship without good communication.

Communication is the process of sharing and receiving information, both verbal and nonverbal, in a manner that accurately conveys intent.

Communication happens on two equally important levels: talking and listening.

My wife runs her own business providing medical care for patients in their homes. I have occasionally gone with her to observe. Once, I watched an elderly couple who had been living together for years. The wife chattered on and on, having a full-blown conversation with herself while her husband sat staring at the TV.

This couple's inability to communicate had probably been going on from the beginning of their relationship. It is difficult to expect a drastic lifestyle change in old age, so if you want to experience healthy communication later in life, you have to start young.

Communication is vital in a marriage. Without it, a marriage will not grow. How can a wife ask for forgiveness when her husband won't listen? How can a husband express his feelings to his wife when she talks incessantly, without allowing him any input in the conversation?

Dishonest Communication

One of the biggest pitfalls in many marriages is not telling the truth about negative feelings. Unfortunately, the greatest deception is often on Sunday mornings. Married couples enter the house of God pretending as if everything is wonderful and perfect at home. My heart goes out to the children of these unions, who see their parents not speaking to one another for the entire week, even while driving to church. Then all of a sudden, when the family enters the foyer, magic occurs. The parents hold hands and chitchat with each other as if nothing's wrong. At that point the children may think, *Praise God, it's a miracle.* Older children will realize their parents are simply hypocrites and may get the message that it is acceptable to be deceptive in church.

Most men are more concerned about how things appear than how things really are, especially when it comes to their marriage. They like to give the impression that their families are stable, their children are well behaved, they have the best jobs and the most envious financial status. When the wife tries to carry the week-long quarrel into the sanctuary, ready to testify to the whole congregation about how unhappy she's been, the husband scrambles to hide the true condition of the marriage. Unfortunately, that only lasts about two hours.

Ultimately, couples need to obey the Scripture that says we are not to let the sun go down on our anger (Ephesians 4:26), meaning we are to resolve issues as soon as they are identified.

Too much focus on looking good leads to a lack of authenticity in our relationships. Personally, I want to know my wife's true feelings because my response depends on what she tells me. I consider it a waste of time and energy for a person to feel one thing and say another. Problems cannot be resolved that way.

The Importance of Listening

Listening demonstrates to your spouse that you care so much about what he has to say, you eliminate all distractions so you can tune in to him.

Not long ago, a wife I know walked into her living room and began to speak to her husband, who was watching TV. The day before, he had learned in his devotional reading that spouses need to listen carefully to each other. So he jumped up, turned off the TV, walked over to his wife, and said, "Honey, I want to hear what you have to say." She was so shocked by the courteous attention, she lost her train of thought.

Communication takes work and selflessness. You become interested in the conversation of someone when you *choose* to do so. If you want your spouse to truly listen to you, demonstrate an interest in the things that are important to him.

James 1:19 says to be quick to listen and slow to speak. Proper listening skills include attitudes of acceptance, respect, and servanthood, even when you don't agree with what is being said.

Many people practice *distracted listening.* They're not really interested in what is being said but act as though they are. Others practice *selective listening,* tuning out based on interest level. Still others practice *arrogant listening,* so threatened by other comments that they shut out any unpleasant messages.

Men tend to listen more closely to sports announcers than to their wives. Three days from now, the game will be forgotten, but your wife will remember whether or not you listened to her.

Ladies should try to keep their conversation balanced and in perspective. If you have a forty-five-minute window for communication, don't spend thirty minutes discussing trivial things that don't build the relationship. Determine what needs to be addressed, and be succinct.

Remember that the last word belongs to God, not either one of you.

Women enjoy listening to the lyrics of romantic love songs crooned by men they don't even know. How much more would they respond to such words from their own husbands?

One way to enhance your listening skills is to involve your entire body. Facial expressions and body language are as important as your words. Make eye contact, face the person who is talking, touch her if appropriate so she can feel comforted while she opens up.

We don't expect success in any other area of our lives without hard work, practice, research, and a game plan. Communication should be treated the same way.

Jesus was a consummate listener. He chose to be interested in all of the disciples. He stayed focused on everything they said. The more He listened, the stronger the bond between them became.

Honest Communication

Quality communication begins with honesty. It's a basic, commonsense idea, but many people fall short at this important step.

When you ask a question, give your spouse the freedom to answer truthfully.

"Honey, does this dress look good on me?" Few men really think there is more than one answer to that question. But if a man doesn't think a dress looks good on his wife, he should be able to tell her so—in love, of course. And wives shouldn't ask such a questions if they don't want to hear the truth.

If there is something wrong, but you don't feel like talking about it, say so. Ephesians 4:25 says, "Laying aside falsehood, speak truth." Don't say, "Nothing's wrong" if something is. If you're not ready to discuss it, simply say, "Let's talk about it later."

Loving Communication

We need to speak words of edification. Proverbs 12:18 says, "There is one who speaks rashly like the thrusts of a sword, but the tongue of the wise brings healing." Ephesians 4:29 says, "Let no unwholesome word proceed from your mouth." This includes those cutting remarks that we practiced as children, then perfected as adults. A sarcastic comment is the surest way to hurt your mate.

Better Communication

There are two key ingredients we tend to neglect when trying to communicate:

1. *Paraphrasing*

A paraphrase is basically a reworded statement of the message you received. Don't address any underlying thoughts behind the message; just tell your partner what you heard him say. If your paraphrase is inaccurate, your mate can resend the message until you accurately understand it.

Paraphrasing helps us to avoid the tendency to make assumptions about our mate's intent. Often, before our partner finishes a statement, we react and respond based on our interpretation.

2. *Validation*

Respect your spouse's opinions. This doesn't mean you will always agree with them. But don't judge your spouse's slant on a situation by refusing to admit that there may be two or more points of view to consider.

Philippians 2:3–4 instructs us to "do nothing from selfishness or empty conceit, but with humility of mind regard one another as more important than yourselves; do not merely look out for your own personal interests, but also for the interests of others."

RESPECTING ONE'S VALUE IN CHRIST

Spouses see each other so "up close and personal," they sometimes don't see their value in God's eyes. A wife may willingly point out her husband's sins, annoying habits, and poor choices but forget that the man she married is more valuable to the Lord than he ever was to her.

Many couples treat perfect strangers better than they treat each other. At a dinner party they are jovial, interested in other people's conversations (no matter how boring), polite, accommodating, and

respectful. Then they drive home giving each other sneers, conde-
scension, eye-rolling, and sometimes completely ignoring each other.

These people have turned a blind eye to their mate's true value.
They focus on what the other person is doing rather than who the
person is. We are all children of God. We are each so valuable to God
that we were purchased with the priceless blood of His Son, Jesus.

Anyone who harms a child of God becomes His enemy. Spouses who cause pain to their mates—whether physically, verbally, or
emotionally—are placing themselves in great jeopardy. God gave
husbands the responsibility to protect their wives, not the power
to control them. Wives are meant to help their husbands, not de-
mean them.

MANAGING CONFLICT

Churches have lost God-fearing, dedicated members because
couples experienced conflict within their marriages, were not sure
how to handle it, and concluded that God must not have been involved in their relationship or they wouldn't be arguing all the time.
But every relationship has conflict. Patients argue with their doctors,
pastors disagree with church members, and employees clash with
their managers. How one deals with the conflict determines how
much or how little pain one experiences.

Conflict can be a good thing. God often uses it to deepen our
relationship with Him and to encourage us to draw closer to His Son.
All too often, however, because of its negative perception and because we are not good at dealing constructively with it, we don't view
conflict as a positive thing. A couple who either avoids disagree-
ments or doesn't manage them properly is cheating themselves out
of a growth opportunity.

UNHEALTHY WAYS TO DEAL WITH CONFLICT

Let's examine some unhealthy ways people choose to handle
conflict.

Deception

One biblical example is revealed in Genesis 27:1–29. In this passage, we see Isaac and Rebecca in a major divergence of opinion concerning their children. Isaac's desire was to bless his elder son, Esau, before his death. Rebecca revealed Isaac's plan to Jacob and encouraged him to use deceit to receive the blessing. Jacob followed her advice and impersonated Esau.

Years later, Jacob's sons, unable to handle their jealousy of their brother Joseph, deceived Jacob. The belief that Joseph had been killed caused Jacob deep grief for many years.

Couples use deception to deal with conflict when they hide money, have an affair, or say they have a headache just to avoid intimacy.

Coalition Formation

Often people align themselves with others to increase their own power. Politicians use this method a lot.

A married couple will sometimes attack each other by using examples of other couples they know, such as deacons, elders, or the financially successful. A wife may give her husband tapes of her favorite sermons to support her position. A husband might quote words from his counselor (often out of context) to support his position and place blame on his wife.

Denial

Some people, for fear of getting the silent treatment or being yelled at, avoid conflict by refusing to acknowledge its existence. This tactic usually fails because the spouse who wants to resolve the disagreement may begin to feel ignored and assume that her feelings and concerns don't count. The spouse employing this tactic is usually perceived as weak.

When a couple is discussing where to go for the family vacation, the type of vehicle they should purchase, or which television program to watch, some people will deny their true preferences in an effort to avoid conflict.

I once counseled a man named Matthew, who was raised in

Nigeria, West Africa. While dating a woman named LaQuita, Matthew occasionally mentioned to her that he preferred meals that were a little spicier than the ones she prepared. His comments were always met with anger and threats to discontinue the relationship. So he finally started saying, "Honey, this food is delicious," regardless of his real opinion. When he wanted the kind of food he preferred, he would sneak out to eat at his African friends' homes.

Issue Expansion

One or both spouses may emphasize issues that are irrelevant to the one being discussed. The objective is to blame the other spouse and try to make him appear oppressive and difficult to deal with. When couples use other problems as ammunition for a present conflict, they never get any closer to resolving it. The goal is to solve the problem, not win a battle.

Yvette and Carl were married for six months when she realized he hadn't been honest about how many times he'd been married prior to his marriage to her. When he was confronted about it in counseling, he started focusing on Yvette's lack of trust with a previous relationship rather than dealing with his own issues.

HEALTHY CONFLICT RESOLUTION

Let's examine some healthy ways of dealing with conflict.

Promptly and Directly

Avoiding conflict with the hope that it will disappear over time does not work. Time alone will not resolve any issue.

Jesse and Sharon had a difficult time adjusting during their first year of marriage. They had both grown up with parents who over-reacted to every little problem. Even though they had not adopted this unhealthy habit, they learned a coping mechanism: silence. This enabled them to get through childhood but caused problems in their marriage.

Sharon became frustrated when Jesse went out with the guys on Friday nights. She thought he was shirking his responsibilities at home, and she resented him for it.

Jesse, on the other hand, couldn't understand why Sharon picked Friday nights to pay bills. He had worked hard all week and wanted to relax for the evening. He figured there was plenty of time on Saturday to take care of mundane tasks.

After three weeks of fuming over her predicament, Sharon expressed her concerns to Jesse. She explained that she wanted to handle their weekly finances early so they could devote their full attention and energy to each other the rest of the weekend. Once Jesse understood where she was coming from, they could discuss a solution.

They decided he could bond with his friends whenever they could get together, but he would come home and pay bills with Sharon before he headed out. That way, Sharon could relax on Friday nights, knowing they were up-to-date on payments and that she'd get quality time with her husband the rest of the weekend.

With Love

Ephesians 4:15 says we must approach confrontation in love. Truth regarding the issue, regardless of whom we perceive to be at fault, must be stated lovingly. Some couples behave self-righteously, condemning and blaming one another in hopes of "winning" the argument. Galatians 6:1 says that when you find a brother at fault, you have the responsibility to approach him gently, lest God allow you to be tempted to do the same thing.

The goal of biblical confrontation is to restore fellowship. Your approach must communicate care and respect.

In Truth

Ephesians 4:25 instructs us to be honest, and that applies to dealing with conflict as well. Don't deny your part in the problem in an attempt to transfer fault to the other person. Proverbs 4:23 instructs us to watch our hearts "with all diligence." Unwholesome words from the mouth reveal an unwholesome state of the heart. If your heart is clean, conflict can be appropriately dealt with. The proper timing, location, setting, and tone will communicate grace.

With Focus

Explain your feelings about the issue. Keep it simple and state the facts. Don't analyze, add, subtract, or choose what you deem important.

Openly

Be willing to give and receive forgiveness. While it is human nature to be competitive, that should be far from your mind if your goal is resolution and peace.

SUMMARY POINTS

✓ Understand God's "instruction manual," the Bible. It is important to understand our roles within the marriage and to recognize God's sovereign role.

✓ We must be willing to invest in our marriages and in our mates. Invest consistently, sacrificially, and be patient for the payoff.

✓ We need to realize the importance of effective, loving communication. This includes talking, listening, and healthy conflict resolution. Without good communication, we jeopardize the very foundation of our marriages.

✓ We should honor our mate's position as a child of God, regularly reminding ourselves that it's not "all about me."

QUESTIONS TO PONDER

Our church recently held a conference for married couples. Our senior pastor, Dr. Tony Evans, and I fielded questions from the conference attendees. Some of the questions we were asked are listed below, along with the answers we gave.

Q. I regret not marrying a committed Christian man. How do I handle my situation?

A. *Pray daily for your husband. Fulfill your biblical role as a godly wife. Encourage any male Christian friends of your husband's to reach out to him. And don't forget that you have to keep growing. Don't be so focused on his shortcomings that you overlook your own spiritual growth.*

Scripture does not allow for divorce based on a spouse not being a believer. If he chooses to stay, you are to stay.

Q. When I got married twenty-five years ago, I was unsaved and so was my husband. Since then I've dedicated my life to Jesus Christ. Now I'm concerned about the expression "What God has put together, let no man put asunder." How could God put me together with my husband when I was unsaved?

A. *God established marriage as a divinely appointed institution for mankind. The moment you entered into your marriage, God recognized and approved of it, regardless of whether you and/or your spouse were believers.*

Q. If marriage is a partnership, shouldn't both partners consult together and consider each other's viewpoints before any major decisions are made?

A. *Yes. The goal is to function as one. After the opinions of both are considered, if the couple still has not reached an agreement, they should spend time praying and fasting about the decision. If the two are still not of one accord, the wife should surrender the decision to the husband since he is the head of the house.*

Q. What should a wife do when she strongly disagrees with a decision made by her husband? Should she do what she knows is right or obey her husband because he is the head?

A. *A godly wife should trust the decision to God unless the matter requires her or her husband to violate Scripture. In that case, the wife is not under obligation to submit to the decision.*

Q. How can a spouse effectively pray for her mate to start tithing? Does God still bless the household if tithes are paid on only one salary?

A. *God honors the heart. If you are doing your part, He will honor you. Continue to pray for your mate to see the importance of this biblical principle.*

Q. Since many women today share in bringing home the income, shouldn't men share in household duties?

A. *The role of the wife is to help her husband. If she is helping him, it is only right for him to help her. One way to approach this is to agree on specific assignments for which each of you is accountable.*

Q. How do I convince my husband to get counseling?

A. *You can't make anyone do anything he doesn't want to. People usually do what makes sense to them. Your job is to lovingly explain to your husband what benefit you think counseling will have in your marriage. If he won't get counseling with you, you may certainly go alone. Choose a counselor your husband will likely respect, and let the counselor decide whether she should contact your husband. Perhaps she will have better success at getting your husband to come to a family session if it's presented in such a way that the husband feels his help is needed to shed light on a situation.*

Q. I've been married for eight years to an angry man. He has no patience with me and is always yelling about something I didn't do right. I'm trying to be obedient to God by staying committed to this marriage, but I don't think I have the strength to stay any longer. What should I do?

A. *Seek counseling. Make sure you have godly people in your life. Realize that you are not responsible for his behavior. You did not cause the anger that dwells inside him. Pray that he will go to anger management therapy, but don't expect him to go on his own. Something drastic may have to happen in his life before he will seek help.*

Q. My husband never compliments me. I compliment him whenever he looks nice and praise him when he does things around the house. I've asked him to do the same for me, but in all the years of our marriage, he has not even tried. What else can I do?

A. *You can tell him that you are hurting because you don't feel valued. You need to realize, however, that what God says about you matters more than what a man may say. All of your needs are met by your heavenly Father. Your sufficiency is in Christ. So be careful not to put too much weight on his compliments. You may desire them, but your world shouldn't come to a halt without them.*

Q. My wife is extremely emotional. She's very negative, worries a lot, and is held captive by circumstances. I want to be the calm in her storm, but I'm confused about how to best do that.

A. *Pray with her every day about the issues in her life. This will draw you closer together as well as help teach her to bring problems to God. If that doesn't work, your wife could be suffering from major depressive disorder characterized by mood swings. She may need to see a mental health professional for an evaluation.*

Q. I have decided to forgive my husband for his affairs in the past, but my feelings don't match up with my decision. How long will this struggle continue?

A. *If he shows the fruit of repentance, which is changed behavior, continue to pray for your husband and work on trusting him again. Over time, feelings generally follow actions. Ask God to bring back your feelings of love for him.*

Q. Why do men think they have the right to sit in their recliners and watch TV while their wives do all the housework? How can I get my husband to help out more?

A. *Most men were raised to believe that their primary responsibility is to go to work and bring home the money, while women are to take care of the home. Even when the woman works, and even if she makes more money, husbands who were raised with that belief system will still struggle with participation in household chores.*

Instead of making a general complaint to your husband that he does not help out around the house enough, ask him to complete specific tasks for you. Try to choose duties that you know he won't mind performing. If he has a problem with something in particular you've requested, ask him if there are any other areas with which he would feel more comfortable helping.

Q. How can I work full-time, raise our kids, cook, wash, clean the house, take care of the yard, pay monthly bills, iron, fold clothes, go to the grocery store, and still have time and energy to be a wife to my husband at bedtime?

A. *Let your husband know that you need help so you can be available to him at night. You may be surprised at how much help you get. If not, you and he may need to evaluate why he is not involved.*

Q. I am in my late forties, and I have no desire for sex. My husband has been very patient with me. How do I get the desire for intimacy back?

A. *First, make sure the problem is not physical. Some sexual struggles can be linked to psychological problems, such as depression. If physical or psychological problems are ruled out, try to meet your husband's sexual needs as much as you can, even if you don't have the desire. Pray together daily that God will return the desire to you.*

In addition, you may need to communicate with your husband some suggestions on how to make your sexual relationship more exciting for you. He may need to be encouraged to express his love through romantic gestures, compliments, words of affection, gentle caresses, soft kisses, etc. Over time his attention to your needs may bring back your desire to meet his.

Q. Shouldn't a wife be allowed to say no to sex without the husband making her feel guilty?

A. *A husband is to show love to his wife by caring for her, not demanding sex. You should not feel guilty because you don't feel like having sex every time he does, especially if you normally seek to meet his needs. Just be sure you are not refusing sex in an attempt to control or punish your husband.*

Q. Every time I touch my wife sexually, she says she's tired. Should a husband beg his wife to have sex?

A. *Try getting cozy at other times when she is not tired. Ask her what you can do to take some of the pressure off so she can get reenergized. A constant excuse of "I'm tired" is usually a sign of marital problems, so you may want to consider counseling, or a trip to the physician's office might be in order to see if her tiredness has any physical connection.*

Q. How do you handle your mate experiencing impotence, but refusing to seek medical help for it?

A. *The inability to perform sexually is an embarrassing problem for most men. So be careful not to shame him through the process. With gentleness and understanding, show him with words of encouragement and acceptance. Your husband also needs to talk with other men who can help him deal with his emotions and encourage him to get treatment. Let him know that getting help would be a loving thing to do because it will enable him to meet your needs.*

4

If you *only* knew...
MY FINANCIAL DIFFICULTIES

Everywhere you go, you see the alluring power of riches. The world constantly tells us that in order to be really satisfied we must have money . . . and lots of it. Ed McMahon tells us, "You may have just won ten million dollars!" Television shows like *Who Wants to be a Millionaire?* may be fun to watch, but the subtle message is that millionaires achieve true happiness.

You might think things would be different among believers in Christ. But we, too, buy into the perception that who we are is based on what we own. We may even go into debt in order to give the perception of affluence. Then, when the bills have piled up and we are no longer able to keep up, we panic. We are afraid of what others will think about our predicament. *What if someone finds out my car is about to be repossessed? How can I face my friends if they discover I don't tithe because I can't afford to? No one else is living paycheck to paycheck like I am.* The insecurities rack up along with the bills.

Once again, the Christian finds himself suffering alone. Few of us are willing to disclose our yearly income, much less the amount we owe. Unless we are prospering financially, people rarely feel comfortable addressing these topics.

Men, particularly, struggle in this area because they are viewed as the primary breadwinners in the home. If they are unable to sufficiently provide for their families, they feel emasculated and embarrassed.

There is no doubt that financial struggles can create stress. Larry Burkett's book entitled *Debt-Free Living: How to Get Out of Debt (And Stay Out)* says, "Nearly 80 percent of divorced couples between the ages of twenty and thirty state their financial problems were the primary cause of their divorce."[1]

Unfortunately, a lot of people make the decision to marry based on finances. When the money runs out, or when the spouse who is the provider starts to limit the supply, marital difficulties follow.

SURFACE CAUSES

People fall into financial difficulties for three basic reasons. First, they don't correctly manage the money they have. They don't establish and stick to a budget. They don't take the time to understand money, invest, save, and organize their finances.

Second, they establish unhealthy comparisons with other people over what each owns. Joe thought that by forty-five, he would have a stable income, two cars (hopefully, one of them a Lexus), and a nice home. But at age forty-five he is struggling to pay his bills. He has a home, but it takes his entire paycheck to keep it running. He has racked up a huge debt, the bank is about to foreclose on his home, the electric company is threatening to shut off the electricity, and he has to somehow come up with enough money to pay for college tuition for his twins, who are graduating high school this year.

"I pay my tithe faithfully," he complains. "I go to church every Sunday. I'm not lazy. I'm working really hard at my job. But McDonald's is the only restaurant I can afford. My unsaved next-door neighbor is living the life I always hoped to have."

Maybe you woke up one day and wondered why you were having so many financial problems. But when you honestly examine your life, you realize that you put yourself into that condition by living way beyond your means. Maybe you've made some foolish decisions in the past. You allowed possessions to define who you are.

Psalm 37:21 says, "The wicked borrows and does not pay back, but the righteous is gracious and gives." It is okay to borrow from the bank, but only if you have the means to pay back.

The third surface cause of financial struggles is the inability to keep a job. Most people have learned how to prepare a résumé and conduct an interview, but lack a healthy work ethic.

THE REAL CAUSES

When people have financial difficulties, there are usually underlying issues that are causing their financial woes.

Tim and Shannon had been married for two years when they came to me for counseling. Both were career oriented. They each owned their own home prior to marriage. But Shannon made approximately $30,000 more than Tim. Because of Shannon's elevated pay, she felt she should be able to do whatever she wanted without consulting her husband, including purchasing a new vehicle and redecorating their home. At face value this couple seemed to have a financial problem. But Shannon's real issue was control.

Sam and Terri were married seven years and had three children. Terri was a school teacher at a local high school and Sam was a self-employed contractor. Finances had always been an issue in their marriage. In the initial stages, they agreed to split the bills and pay them separately. But Sam never paid the electric bill on time, which led to the lights being disconnected. Terri felt frustrated because Sam "is irresponsible and doesn't care about his family." Terri was late on her portion of the mortgage because she had to pay for dental work for their six-year-old, and their home was in danger of foreclosure. These situations created a lack of trust, but they were not willing to change their arrangement. Terri felt frustrated about Sam's lack of responsibility, and he was annoyed with her constant nagging about money. Again, Sam and Terri didn't really have a money problem. Their problem stemmed from the decision to live separate financial lives. Independent decisions they made regarding finances created other problems. They had to take a serious look at those decisions that were not working and change them.

Charles and Sandy were married for twenty-five years. They had four children. Charles was a high-profile lawyer, and Sandy was a stay-at-home mom. Sandy had studied nursing but never completed her degree. Charles gave Sandy approximately $100 a week to live on. She had to ask him for money to buy groceries, gas, and other expenses. Any purchases she wanted for herself had to come from her "allowance." Because Sandy was a Christian, she did not think it was her place to say anything to Charles regarding money.

Charles ruled his home with an iron first. His children had to pay for their college costs if they did not receive scholarships or grants. Loans were unacceptable. Charles often spent money on golf, cars, and traveling.

In counseling, Charles realized he did not want his wife to have too much money because he feared she might become self-sufficient and leave him, as his mother did his father. Charles and Sandy needed to examine their belief system about money. A new biblical belief system needed to be put in place.

LOOKING AT MONEY REALISTICALLY

Money doesn't heal your pains or fix your problems. It is not a true source of happiness. When you get it, you only want more.

The False Prophets

Some preachers claim that God wants His people to be rich. They point to Philippians 4:19, which says, "And my God will supply all your needs according to His riches in glory in Christ Jesus."

"Then," you may ask, "why do others prosper more than I do? Does that mean I'm not spiritual?"

First Timothy 6:8 says we should be content if we simply have "food and covering." Philippians 4:19 states that God will supply all of our *needs,* not our wants.

Poor people abounded during Christ's days. Jesus said we will always have the poor among us. (See Matthew 26:11; Mark 14:7; John 12:8.)

What Scripture Says

First Timothy 6:7 says, "For we have brought nothing into the world, so we cannot take anything out of it either." Everything you have will be left with someone else when you leave this world. The only way money can impact eternity is by impacting hearts. If we allow money to rule us, we will have to make an account for it one day. But if we view money as a means to bless others and provide for their needs, we will have eternal rewards.

Is it wrong to be rich? No. But we are not to desire to be rich for the sake of being rich, or to demand prosperity from God.

OUR ATTITUDE TOWARD MONEY

First Timothy 6:9 reads, "But those who want to get rich fall into temptation and a snare and many foolish and harmful desires which plunge men into ruin and destruction." This verse does not say "those who are rich," but rather, "those who want to get rich." The reason for our existence is to glorify God, whether we have great wealth or not. If it is the desire of your heart to gain wealth, you have to seriously consider why you want to be wealthy. You may say, "If I were rich, I'd give more to the church." Maybe. Maybe not.

If God gives you an excess, you are to use it for His glory. Proverbs 10:22 says, "It is the blessing of the Lord that makes rich, and He adds no sorrow to it." So if God allows your business to prosper, praise Him! If you are making an average salary, praise Him! God's will is that you be content with what He gives you. If you have a good understanding of finances and have put money in its proper place, you will tend to be more generous with what you have rather than complain about what you don't have.

In Luke 12:16–21, Jesus told a parable about a man whose land "was very productive." In fact, the man had such a good year he had no place to store all his goods. "This is what I will do," he said. "I will tear down my barns and build larger ones, and there I will store all my grain and my goods. And I will say to my soul, 'Soul, you have many goods laid up for many years to come; take your ease, eat, drink and be merry' " (verses 18–19). God gave the man excess to bless him so the man could, in turn, be a blessing to others. But the man did not realize that what he received was a blessing from the Lord. He did not give proper credit to the One who had given him the blessing.

In Genesis 12:2 the Lord told Abram He was going to bless him and his seed. "And I will make you a great nation, and I will bless you, and make your name great; *and so you shall be a blessing*" (italics mine). God was going to bless the nation of Israel so they could bless others. It isn't wrong to spend a little money on yourself as long as you have the right attitude. However, if God places it on your heart to give to someone who is in need, and He blesses you with excess to do so, He expects you to use it for the purpose He intends.

When you are generous with others, God will be generous with you. Luke 6:36 says, "Be merciful, just as your Father is merciful." The result is described two verses later: "Give, and it will be given to you. They will pour into your lap a good measure—pressed down, shaken together, and running over. For by your standard of measure it will be measured to you in return."

Some people actually come to church to get rich. They may join a relatively large congregation just to get business connections. It is not wrong to benefit from business deals with fellow believers. But attending church primarily for financial gain is not God's way.

Paul says in Philippians 4:11–12, "Not that I speak from want, for I have learned to be content in whatever circumstances I am. I know how to get along with humble means, and I also know how to live in prosperity; in any and every circumstance I have learned the secret of being filled and going hungry, both of having abundance and suffering need." Paul had learned to not let his financial situation control him. Money is a gift of God's grace. Nothing we have is really ours. God gave it to us, and He can take it back whenever He wants. We are simply stewards.

Habakkuk 3:17–18 tells of Habakkuk's desire to truly know God. "Though the fig tree should not blossom and there be no fruit on the vines, though the yield of the olive should fail and the fields produce no food, though the flock should be cut off from the fold and there be no cattle in the stalls, yet I will exult in the Lord, I will rejoice in the God of my salvation." Habakkuk knew what it meant to be content in God alone. Even if all means of financial gain were cut off, he would be content just being with God.

SPIRITUAL REFERENCES

Ezekiel 18:7–9 says, "If a man does not oppress anyone, but restores to the debtor his pledge . . . he is righteous and will surely live." (Please note: This Scripture also lists other tasks that need to be completed in order to be considered righteous, including walking in God's statutes.)

"If anyone does not provide for his own, and especially for those of his household, he has denied the faith and is worse than an unbeliever" (1 Timothy 5:8).

"He who loves money will not be satisfied with money, nor he who loves abundance with its income" (Ecclesiastes 5:10).

"The sleep of the working man is pleasant, whether he eats little or much; but the full stomach of the rich man does not allow him to sleep" (Ecclesiastes 5:12).

"But godliness actually is a means of great gain when accompanied by contentment. For we have brought nothing into the world, so we cannot take anything out of it either. If we have food and covering, with these we shall be content. But those who want to get rich fall into temptation and a snare and many foolish and harmful desires which plunge men into ruin and destruction. For the love of money is a root of all sorts of evil, and some by longing for it have wandered away from the faith and pierced themselves with many griefs" (1 Timothy 6:6–10).

SUMMARY POINTS

- ✔ Some people are so obsessed with acquiring money they live beyond their means to appear that they are financially well-off.

- ✔ People with money problems usually have underlying issues or beliefs that are the root cause.

- ✔ God promised to supply our needs, not our wants. We must learn to be grateful for the provisions the Lord has made for us.

- ✔ Prosperity is not a sin. Our attitude about financial status and possessions is critical.

- ✔ When God blesses us monetarily, we should look for ways to be a blessing to others.

QUESTIONS TO PONDER

- ✔ What do I think having money will do for me? Are there problems that I believe would disappear if only I had "enough" money?

- ✔ Am I living within my means? Or am I convinced that I must match my neighbors' acquisitions?

- ✔ What do I think God's attitudes are toward money, wealth, and prosperity? What Scriptures do I know that can speak to this?

✓ When I am blessed with increase, do I think about ways in which I can use the money, or how it can be used to benefit others?

5

If you *only* knew...
My Sexual Pain

Many Christians today have been wounded because of inappropriate sexual encounters and their inability to confront desires of the flesh. Proverbs 6:27 says, "Can a man take fire in his bosom and his clothes not be burned?"

Unfortunately the topic of sex is often swept under the rug within the family of believers. Therefore, people who struggle with sexual issues quickly discover that the church is unwilling to help them. They are left to try to manage their pain on their own.

Human beings are, by nature, sexual creatures. Physical sex is one of the most intimate ways you can tell your spouse that you love him or her. God created sex in order for a husband and wife to be united as one. It is meant to be enjoyed. When God is at the center of our lives, sex can be one of the richest and most wonderful experiences we can have. However, sex has become perverted and distorted by self-centeredness.

Satan always tries to steal what God has given. The enemy has done a great job of deceiving us when it comes to sex. The world has become bathed in immorality because of our culture's insatiable desires. Sexually explicit material is more accessible than ever with the invention of the Internet.

Since our culture has become so engrossed in immorality, Christians can become caught up in it too. Even hugging in the church can be inappropriate if the motives spring from sexual frustration or manipulation.

Many believers struggle with sexual issues but don't know what to do about it. They certainly can't admit their problem to anyone. After all, Christians are supposed to be spiritual. We can't let anyone know about our pain.

PAST SEXUAL PAIN

Over the past fifteen years, I have had the opportunity to minister to several men and women who struggle with sexual pain. Early in my practice I was aghast at the number of people who were abused as children.

The Pain of Abuse

In 2000, the National Violence Against Women Prevention Research Center reported that "in a national survey of adolescents, 13% of females and 3.4% of males reported being sexually assaulted before the age of 18." This organization estimates that "one in four women and one in seven men report a history of some form of childhood sexual abuse." Most offenders are people familiar with and/or related to the child. In almost 40 percent of child abuse cases, the perpetrator is a nonrelative whom the child knows; 16 percent of abusers are a parent or stepparent.[1]

A childhood tarnished by sexual pain can lead to an adult lifestyle of promiscuity, homosexuality, or abusing others.

The Pain of Homosexuality

Homosexuality is one way that abuse manifests itself. Many people who identify themselves as "gay" were sexually abused as children or adolescents. A painful past often leads to confusion with gender roles.

A friend of mine (we'll call him Jay) told me he was sexually molested at the age of five by his church's choir director. As a result of that abuse, Jay became confused about his sexual orientation. He ended up abusing other young men and engaging in a bisexual lifestyle. Eventually he contracted AIDS and died from it. If he had not been abused at that early stage of his life, Jay might be alive today.

Issues of sexual orientation have become prominent in today's society. Because homosexuality is considered less taboo than in previous years, people feel more comfortable discussing their unconventional sexual activities.

Of all the struggles addressed in this book, I would venture to say that homosexuality is still the biggest secret within the church. As a whole, the religious community seems to find same-sex physical relations the most distasteful and disobedient of all the sins.

It is no wonder, then, that those who practice homosexuality feel the church has turned its back on them. Gay people feel judged and alienated, and church members are at a loss as to how to act toward them.

There is a heated debate over whether gay people are "born that way" (biologically oriented to sexual behavior) or if they learn the behavior through past painful experiences.

To say that homosexuality is biological would be equivalent to saying that God placed that burden on them. In Romans 1:26–27, the Word of God describes the homosexual relationship as men and women abandoning and exchanging the natural function for the unnatural. This makes the decision to enter into an unnatural relationship a person's choice, not God's.

The church finds itself in a quandary about how to deal with this issue. On one hand, the Bible clearly indicates that it is a sin, and like all sin, it should not be condoned. On the other hand, believers are instructed to set a Christlike example and show love to those who sin.

The solution, of course, is to separate sinful behavior (the things a person does) from the person who commits the sin. We can hate the sin, yet still extend compassion toward the person who practices it.

It is impossible to recognize and heal the pain of those around us if we turn our backs on them. No one comes to Christ because someone judged her into it. We give our lives to the Lord because we feel loved, not despised; welcomed, not rejected.

How, then, should we respond to someone who confesses he is gay? In the same manner as any other sin. We acknowledge how difficult it must have been for this person to admit his secret. We tell him we appreciate his sharing the truth with us. And we welcome him into the fold. This is what we do with alcoholics, smokers, thieves, liars, and adulterers. Homosexuals should be no different.

The Pain of Abusing Others

It may be difficult to believe that a person who commits sexual abuse is suffering, but that is usually the case. Abusers are commonly victims themselves. They grew up feeling powerless and worthless. As an adult, they try to regain a sense of control by inflicting pain on others, acting out the same scenarios they experienced when they were younger.

An abuser always chooses victims who are powerless and unlikely to report the abuse, such as young children. He cannot relate to adults in a healthy way, so he has no truly loving relationships.

People who have committed abuse and who have not been rehabilitated become a danger to those around them. If someone you know is abusing others, it is imperative that action be taken to stop the abuse. You may have to report the individual to the police, testify in court, or take some other drastic measure to protect the interests of the victim.

Compassion does not mean passivity. While it is certainly compassionate to offer prayer for an individual who is abusing, getting personally involved demonstrates love toward the victim as well as the abuser. Without the threat of punishment, abusers usually don't have any reason to seek help to start changing their behavior.

The Pain of Promiscuity

People who were abused as children often end up equating sex with love. They think the only way to show love is to have sex; after all, the abuser (usually a trusted family member or friend) "loved" them in that manner.

Abuse victims may choose to be promiscuous as a means of reclaiming power over their lives.

Vanessa was date raped in her freshman year of college. She spent the next two years actively pursuing sexual relationships with various men. She determined that she would decide whom she slept with, when, and how often. Vanessa dropped out of college when she became pregnant by one of her "conquests." Until she came to me for counseling, Vanessa never connected her date rape to her sexual acting out.

The Pain of Lost Trust

Pain resulting from inappropriate or unhealthy relationships often results in an inability to trust. A single woman may think, *Are there really any men out there who won't hurt me?* A married woman may wonder if she can even trust the preacher. *He probably abuses his wife or cheats on her like my husband did.*

DEALING WITH PAST SEXUAL PAIN

People who are struggling with issues from their past do not need to suffer forever. Their lives can get better.

The first step toward healing is learning to forgive. Victims of sexual abuse need to start by forgiving themselves. They need to understand that they didn't do anything to cause this horrible thing to happen. There is no need to feel guilty about what they could have done differently. Abusers are sick people, and sometimes their illness spills over to those around them.

Healing from sexual abuse also requires forgiving the offender. (This subject is addressed in depth in the chapter on Bitterness.)

Even those who are suffering from the consequences of their own choices need to forgive themselves. This can be challenging to do, especially if you have a daily reminder of your poor decision: a young child to raise, a sexually transmitted disease, or friends who practice the behavior you are trying to separate yourself from.

Christ granted the ultimate pardon. He forgave us for all our sins before we were even a twinkle in our parents' eyes! Since He knew the mistakes we would make and chose to accept us despite them, should we not forgive as well? Our judgment of ourselves and others should not be more severe than our Creator's.

Once you've accepted the Lord's forgiveness, you are no longer in bondage to those sins. Who you were in the past is not who you must continue to be. Through Christ, you have the power to make better choices for your life.

I'm not saying that all you have to do is shoot up a quick prayer and your problems will miraculously disappear. Healing usually requires long, hard work. But God is gracious enough to provide us with ways to manage the consequences of our past.

You must seek Him, and watch for His solutions. For example, you could look for a support group or read books that apply to your situation. You may also wish to speak with a pastor or counselor who can help you gain perspective on your past and offer suggestions for dealing appropriately with it.

DEALING WITH PRESENT SEXUAL PAIN

Sexual issues can cause so much embarrassment and fear of misunderstanding that those who struggle with them may avoid the church—the very place where healing can best take place.

The Pain of Pornography

I recently counseled a couple named Byron and Vicki, who had been married for nine years and had two children. Byron was considering ending the marriage because he believed Vicki no longer cared for him

"For the past six years," he stated, "she hasn't initiated sex once. If I don't make a move, we don't make love. So, I've given up. I pay the bills and make repairs around the house, but that's it. It's like having a roommate instead of a wife. Some people have suggested I hook up with another woman, but I know that won't solve the problem."

"I don't understand what the big deal is," Vicki said. "I work a full-time job, take care of the kids, and keep our house in order. By the end of the day, I'm simply tired. Besides, I was raised to believe that it's not a woman's place to initiate sexual contact."

"It feels like you don't want me," Byron said.

"I never deny you when you approach me sexually," Vicki replied. "If I didn't want you, I wouldn't do it."

"You know, I've rarely seen her unclothed in the nine years we've been married," Byron told me. "She even expects me to put a towel over myself as soon as I get out of the shower."

"I'm uncomfortable about my body," Vicki admitted. "So I guess I've always assumed he wouldn't like it either."

Knowing that a lack of body confidence is one of the results of sexual abuse, I asked Vicki if she had ever been abused. She replied firmly that she had not.

After several more counseling sessions, however, Vicki revealed to me that some years prior, she had been date raped. She decided not to tell Byron about her experience because she didn't want him to think she had any deep issues. Besides, she was convinced that Byron's love would eventually cause her memory of the assault to fade away. Obviously, it did not. It simply caught up with her when she least expected it.

One of the ways Byron had chosen to cope with his wife's unresponsiveness was pornography. I told him to get rid of it immediately. This couple had young, impressionable children, and his behavior could negatively impact their psyches. In addition, pornography was harming his marriage. Vicki already had a negative body image. How could she improve it, knowing her husband was looking at pictures of women with unrealistically "perfect" physiques?

When Byron finally acknowledged that his pornography habit was a problem, he made a commitment to stop. He and Vicki are still in therapy, but they are making tremendous progress both individually and as a couple.

The Pain of Adultery

Another source of pain for people in churches today is the sin of adultery. When a betrayed mate discovers the deception, she may start to wonder, *Should I file for divorce? Or just kill him and spend the rest of my life in jail?* Concern for the children, feelings of failure, and fear of financial disaster can lead to the faithful spouse thinking, *Maybe I should retaliate by having an affair myself. It seems like everyone else is.*

When a person discovers that his spouse is cheating, he will be confused, angry, hurt, and vengeful. Despite these emotions, the appropriate next step is to collect all the relevant facts so he can understand exactly what is going on. He needs to confront his spouse candidly. Try to determine if the unfaithful spouse has a problem that needs to be addressed, or if this was a one-time mistake for which she is truly repentant.

If the affair is one of many, or there is a significant underlying issue, the faithful spouse will need to determine his own limits and level of comfort. Will he stand by his mate and be a source of support while she gets help? Or does he need to remove himself from the relationship while she seeks help on her own? There is no right or wrong answer. Each person needs to do what he feels comfortable with and what he thinks would best benefit the relationship.

On the other hand, if the adulterous spouse made a one-time mistake, Galatians 6:1 applies: "Brethren, even if anyone is caught in any trespass, you who are spiritual, restore such a one in a spirit of gentleness." Forgiveness can be a challenge, but everyone makes mistakes. A heart that forgives can also restore.

THE RESULTS OF SEXUAL PAIN

Sexual pain can impact a person's view of God. You may wonder why God didn't keep the abuser away. Or why He didn't stop your spouse from cheating on you. Or why He doesn't simply remove inappropriate sexual thoughts from your mind.

It is human nature to wonder where God is when tragedy strikes. But He hasn't turned His back on you. Nor has He overlooked your circumstance. We live in a sinful world, and we are subject to its impact. That is the cost of free will. But our Father can use any situation for His glory and for the benefit of His children.

Romans 8:28 says, "And we know that God causes all things to work together for good to those who love God, to those who are called according to His purpose."

In Genesis 37:23–28, God allowed Joseph's brothers to throw him into a pit and then sell him to a group of traveling slave traders. Joseph must have wondered why the Lord did not stop this inexcusable abuse, especially when he went from slavery to imprisonment even though he had done nothing wrong.

But God had a plan. He wanted to put Joseph in a position where he could rescue his people—including his brothers and their families—from a famine that was about to devastate the land. When the brothers realized that their very survival depended on the young man they had abused years before, they humbled themselves before Joseph and begged for his forgiveness.

The sins of Joseph's brothers did not stop God from extending mercy to them as well. He allowed the very object of their jealousy to save their lives.

WHAT CAN WE DO?

Why don't Christians recognize the sexual pain in their churches and do something about it? Some church members have not worked through their own issues, so they don't know how to help others. Others may be abusers themselves. Most people are simply unaware of the problem. Unfortunately, many in our congregations today are not willing to get involved in the personal lives of their fellow parishioners.

Take Responsibility for Your Actions

Second Samuel 11 tells the story of David and Bathsheba. It would have been easy for David to say, "I couldn't help having sex with that beautiful woman. She was right there on her rooftop naked. Didn't she know she was tempting me? One look at her and I couldn't help myself."

But David never said this. In Psalm 51:3–4, David confessed his sin. "For I know my transgressions, and my sin is ever before me. Against You, You only, I have sinned and done what is evil in Your sight, so that You are justified when You speak and blameless when You judge."

Whom did David blame for his sin? Himself.

It is easy to blame our sin on other people or circumstances in our past or present. Our mother did not raise us properly. We didn't have a father in the home to give us a proper role model. We grew up in too much poverty . . . or too much affluence.

Some men blame women for the way they dress. True, it would help men's struggle tremendously if women would dress modestly. But men are the ones who undressed them mentally.

It's true, sin does have contributing factors. But ultimately, the decision falls on us. We need to stop blaming other things and other people and deal with the true source of sin: ourselves. Circumstances may accelerate our actions, but they are still our actions.

Know Where You Are Weak

Frank knew he had a problem with lust. His drive to work included going through an area filled with bars advertising adult entertainment, and he often found himself tempted to check them out. He could have taken an alternate route, but that meant ten extra minutes of driving.

Frank thought it was safe to get close to temptation. After all, he figured, he was strong enough to pass it up. He didn't realize he was playing with fire.

After a few weeks of driving past these bars, Frank stopped at one on the way home and went inside. He only lingered in the doorway for a few minutes, but what he saw was enough to arouse his lust. When he arrived home, a little later than usual, he had trouble looking his wife in the eye.

From that day on, Frank started taking the longer way home from work.

Frank took one more step in overcoming his temptation. He confessed that he had a problem. He sought out resources, organizations, and books that addressed sexual temptation. He created a strong support system for himself through an accountability partner and a small group of close friends with whom he could share his daily struggles. He threw himself into God's Word and prayer.

It wasn't easy, but Frank eventually overcame his lust stronghold. He learned to distinguish a healthy sex drive from a destructive one. Now he avoids putting himself in situations that weaken him. His wife is thrilled because his behavior honors both her and God.

Seek Help

Most people are reluctant to discuss the deeply personal issues with which they are struggling. The majority of people who have sexual pain do not even admit they have a problem until something forces them to do so.

A woman who has had numerous sexual partners doesn't take abstinence seriously until she contracts a sexually transmitted disease. A man thinks his marital affairs are harmless until his wife gathers up the kids and moves out of the house. A sex offender doesn't stop until one of his victims reports the crime and presses charges. People often have to lose something precious to them before they realize they need to get their lives in order.

When we finally find the courage to repent of our sins and change our behavior, the most important resource we can have is compassionate, loving, sensitive people who are willing to support us. If you are suffering from sexual pain, past or present, find someone you can talk to and ask for help.

And remember, God still loves you. He can see you through your battle. No matter how dismal the circumstances, there is always hope for healing when our heavenly Father is involved.

Help Others

If someone approaches you with a declaration of his sexual sin, be receptive to your friend's struggles. Do not judge or condemn him, but offer support and encouragement to the best of your ability. If his needs exceed your resources, offer to help this wounded friend find professional guidance.

The Bible says we are all born into sin. Our churches need to develop counseling ministries where people who are gifted in the area of caring and nurturing can be taught how to help those in need from a biblical frame of reference. Every church should train its congregation to be sensitive and loving enough to confront and encourage those who are struggling sexually. One-on-one accountability relationships should be developed within the body.

Every new member could be matched with someone who is trained to ask difficult questions regarding life issues. If the new member indicates a desire to deal with certain problems, he or she could be referred to the counseling center.

If you know someone who is suffering from sexual pain, allow God's love to motivate you into action. You may be able to counsel, support, listen, or simply refer that person to some useful resources that can get him on track. Always be open to the tasks to which God may call you. Even if you feel uncomfortable or unqualified, allow Him to do His good work through you, and you will be blessed as you bless others.

SUMMARY POINTS

✓ Men and women alike struggle with sexual frustration. Our pews are filled with people who are not dealing with their pain.

✓ Sexual pain is one of the most destructive issues in relationships. Churches need to develop ministries designed to help people in pain.

✓ No one is immune to temptation, and none of us is strong enough to resist it on our own. We need one another, and the power of the Holy Spirit, to keep us strong.

QUESTIONS TO PONDER

✓ Why am I resistant to seeking help with my sexual pain?

✓ Do I feel as though I am the only one going through this type of problem?

✓ Do I really think my painful situation will go away if I continue to keep it a secret?

✓ Do I try to help others who are in pain, but avoid seeking help for myself?

6

If you *only* knew...
My Addiction

Christians tend to be either compassionate or judgmental toward addiction depending on the object of the addiction. Many of us can relate to a food addict who succumbs to gluttony during stressful times. Addictions to cigarettes or shopping are also treated lightly. But alcohol, drugs, and sex are a different story.

Few churches have ministries that are equipped to deal with such problems. So struggling believers are left to suffer in silence and solitude.

John 8:36 reads, "If the Son makes you free, you will be free indeed." I think of this Scripture whenever the word *addiction* is mentioned.

Addiction is a form of bondage. It binds you against your will like a prisoner behind bars. The prisoner can't just walk out of the jail whenever he feels like it. He needs someone to release him in order for him to be free.

Webster[1] defines the word *addict* as "to give oneself up to a strong habit; to cause to become addicted or hooked; one addicted and fix-ated to a habit, such as using drugs, or a certain behavior." One of my clients said of his addiction to alcohol, "I could stop, but I couldn't stay stopped."

I believe addiction is an emotional disease. Many people start out thinking they can break their habit at will. But when addiction takes root, life becomes unmanageable.

A man buys nude magazines. Next, he watches soft porn on the cable channel. Then, when he goes on business trips, he watch-es X-rated movies in his room.

A woman overeats a little to comfort herself after a divorce. She continues the behavior, and before long she is thirty pounds over-weight. Her clothes don't fit any longer, so she becomes discouraged. She can't stand to look at herself in the mirror because she doesn't recognize her own body. To comfort herself, she eats more.

Since this is not a book about addiction, but on the pain we try to hide, I will take a general approach to this subject but will make some specific suggestions on how to deal with it.

WHAT IS ADDICTION?

Addiction is any impulsive, habitual behavior that has taken root in our lives and become difficult to shake. It happens when we feel that we just can't do without something. We have to get our "fix," and we will do whatever it takes to satisfy our desire.

Addiction is actually idolatry. It becomes so important to us, we must bow to it. The focus of our addiction becomes the foremost object of our affection. It prevents us from freely loving God and oth-ers because we have "tunnel vision," concerned primarily with hav-ing our addictive needs met.

I had a client named Heidi who was in denial about her mari-juana use. She tried to convince herself that she didn't have a prob-lem and that her habit didn't affect her relationship with God. But one day Heidi said to me, "I've come to realize that I'm just fooling myself. I have a problem in my walk with God. I want to pray and read my Bible, but I can't because I stay so high all the time."

We give our addiction the time, energy, and resources that God and our family deserve. When Christ was asked what the greatest commandment is, He quoted Deuteronomy 6:4–6, "Hear, O Israel! The Lord is our God, the Lord is one! You shall love the Lord your God with all your heart and with all your soul and with all your might." The greatest commandment is to love our Lord with all our hearts. Like idolatry, addiction interferes with our worship of God.

OBJECTS OF ADDICTION

Usually, when people think of addiction, they focus primarily on alcohol or drugs. But addiction can come in other forms, such as food, sex, work, gambling, and shopping. Our pews are full of people who have succumbed to various addictions. Most of us suffer from addiction on some level.

I have been accused of being a workaholic because I enjoy working six days a week. Although an "addiction" to work cannot compare to being an alcoholic or a drug abuser, I sometimes experience the same spiritual and neurological dynamics they do. It is the degree of focus on a habit that can take it across the line from a healthy interest to an addiction. We can love something like work as long as it doesn't take the place of God or our families.

A behavior is addictive when we are blind to the fact that our fixation erodes our free will, destroys our dignity, and dictates our behavior.

Addiction to People

Second Samuel 13 tells the story of Amnon, the son of David, and his sister Tamar. Tamar was extremely beautiful. Amnon was in love with her and longed for her. "Amnon was so frustrated because of his sister Tamar that he made himself ill, for she was a virgin, and it seemed hard to Amnon to do anything to her" (verse 2). Amnon was obsessed with Tamar. He wanted his sister so badly that he literally became sick over it. Physical pain and discomfort because one can't have the object upon which one is fixated is a common symptom of addiction.

Amnon deceived his sister into thinking he just wanted some loving care. Tamar thought she was nursing her sick brother back to health, but all the while Amnon was contriving to have sex with her. His manipulative behavior indicates that his sexual desire was controlling him.

Addiction to Activities

For the past fifteen years, I've worked closely with three kinds of addicts: the alcoholic, the cocaine addict, and the sex addict. I've seen how destructive these people can be to themselves and their loved ones.

In their book *Dying for a Drink,*[2] authors Anderson M. D. Spickard and Barbara R. Thompson describe the problem:

> For the alcohol addict, the problem never ends. The alcoholic is an individual who cannot predict when he will drink or how much he will drink, and who continues to drink even after alcohol causes him trouble in one or more areas of life—family, friends, health, job, finances, legal matters and so on. Unlike the alcohol abuser, the alcohol addict is no longer in control of his own will. His internal center for decision making and free choice has been captured by alcohol and he is unable to choose not to drink.

Alcoholics can always give reasons for their drinking, such as "I need to get through the day," or "I have no intention of getting drunk."

I counseled Michael, who was struggling with cyber sex addiction. His wife, Angie, threatened for six months to divorce him. She was attempting to get him to see how his behavior was affecting her and their family.

Michael spent so much time on the computer he rarely got any sleep. Since he had a computer at work, Angie was sure that was a temptation for him as well. She feared that his habit would impact his work performance and jeopardize his job.

For months, Michael came to our sessions claiming that the only reason his "hobby" was a problem was because his wife didn't like him doing it. According to him, it wasn't the worst sin in the world. If he wasn't doing that, he argued, he'd probably find something else to do.

During the time I counseled Michael, the government was arresting people for participating in Internet child pornography. As a matter of fact, Michael knew one of the people who was arrested. This changed the course of our discussions. He began to recognize that his behavior might be a problem.

Michael promised me and his wife that he would stop. But, with any addiction, the road to recovery can be a long, difficult one. After about a month he was back at it. It wasn't until Michael stopped blaming, rationalizing, and spiritualizing his problem that he was able to start recovering from his addiction.

We live in a society where enduring any form of pain has become unacceptable. We want a quick fix to the uncomfortable situations we face, forgetting that pain is sometimes a necessary part of life.

As a society, we have become weak. We drink, smoke, gamble, shop, work, and eat our troubles away. But these activities cannot solve our problems. Persevering through trials builds character.

THE ADDICTION PROCESS

The process of addiction begins inside a person. As the addiction takes over, it begins to impact other people's lives both directly and indirectly.

The Changes Within

No one sets out to become an addict or considers it a personal achievement. Most people don't see it coming.

When I was twelve, my father, who drank occasionally, decided to let me try alcohol. He thought, *If I don't let him taste this, he might do it elsewhere.* So he offered me a small amount of stout beer and watched me take a sip. It put such an awful taste in my mouth, I immediately left the room to brush my teeth.

How, I wondered, could my father like this stuff? I took a few more sips, determined that I was going to drink stout beer like my dad. I had long admired the way he relaxed and enjoyed a drink with friends; it seemed such a manly thing to do. But that beer tasted just as horrible the second time around as it did the first, so that was the extent of my drinking. Still, my father's willingness to consume alcohol clearly sent a message to me that drinking was acceptable.

Families play an influential role as a child's first societal environment; therefore, it is important for parents to be careful about the behaviors they demonstrate. Children naturally admire their parents and are quick to emulate their behavior.

Chemical dependency usually begins with recreational drug use that started during childhood or adolescence. Difficulties at home or school can lead a child to attempt to deal with those challenges in an inappropriate way with peers outside the home. During adulthood, alcohol and drugs are introduced as coping mechanisms to get through stressful situations like divorce, losing a job, problems with rearing a child, personal tragedy, or some unmet expectation.

Just as some medical conditions like diabetes, cancer, and heart problems run in the family, so does the predisposition toward chemical addiction. Children of drug and alcohol addicts are more likely to attempt to use those substances. But just because someone may be predisposed to addiction, that does not mean he will become an addict. The individual's social environment, faith, and personal determination all play major roles as well.

Many addicts blame their families and the environment. Those factors may contribute to the situation, but the ultimate decision to overindulge is solely the individual's. Only when an addict accepts personal responsibility can recovery begin.

Many people who are addicted have other issues they are masking through the use of the substance. Sometimes they are aware of those issues, but often they are not.

A woman may suffer from anxiety or depression that has not been diagnosed but which contributes to her addiction. She uses drugs as an escape from her depression. Because the relief is temporary, she continues to indulge. She now has a dual diagnosis: depression and addiction.

Usually addicts do not realize when their consumption increases. Over time a habit gets out of control and becomes an addition. The addict is unable to see the destructive relationship between his behavior and the consequences of that behavior. Denial blinds him to his illness. It tells him there is no problem; therefore, there is no need to deal with it.

If the addict doesn't completely deny having a problem, he may minimize its severity by convincing himself it is under control. These rationalizations accomplish nothing. Until a person admits to having a problem, he can't even begin to overcome it. That is why the first stage in a twelve-step program is for a person to admit he has a problem he can't manage on his own.

Once the problem is acknowledged, it is common for an addict to discount the negative consequences. These consequences must usually be communicated to the addict by people close to her. A compulsive shopper may hear complaints from her family that she is overlooking some of her responsibilities. Her husband may notice that bills are not being paid on time, and when he asks, she confesses that she doesn't have enough money to pay them. She forgets to do household chores. She may neglect to pick up the children from day care or her husband from work.

Those in big trouble will usually make statements like:

- "I can stop when I want to, but I just don't want to right now."
- "It's not as bad as you're making it seem."
- "I made a little mistake. Don't act like you've never forgotten to do something."
- "So I drink a little too much on occasion. You eat too much."
- "The laws regarding marijuana are stupid. After all, physicians prescribe it for medicinal purposes."

Addicts who rationalize a particular habit are "externalizing" the behavior, trying to cast blame outside themselves. As long as they can blame the nagging wife, the abusive husband, the crazy mother-in-law, the stupid legal system, the controlling boss, the ill-mannered child, or the judgmental friend, they don't have to look at themselves. As long as they remain in this state of mind, there is no way for them to get better.

The Impact on Others

During a moment of clarity, an addict will seem to understand how his addiction has impacted his life and his loved ones. He may have been a senior-level executive, the one everybody in the company looked to for advice and direction. At home he was the backbone of his family, the dream husband, the one most likely to succeed. He earned prestigious awards and perhaps even went on speaking engagements around the country to discourage students from using drugs. He was charming and friendly, and he loved the Lord.

But he became increasingly unrecognizable to his loved ones. He was aware of the pain he was causing others. He saw the disappointment in their eyes. From time to time he took inventory of his life and considered what it could have been like without his destructive behavior.

But just as denial affects the ability to see and deal with the truth, a process called *euphoric recall* plays a trick on the mind of an addict.

Euphoric recall allows the addict to remember the great feelings they experienced before, during, and shortly after participating in the addictive behavior. They are drawn back to the experience because they think only about feeling happy, empowered, content, or excited. A corresponding feeling of anxiety is associated with not participating in the behavior. "If I don't have a drink before this party, I won't be relaxed enough to have a good time."

Euphoric recall ignores the fact that the addict just got out of jail for driving under the influence or for stealing.

Family members are usually conflicted about how to help a loved one who is addicted. I usually ask them to disconnect their emotions from the situation and evaluate the effectiveness of their efforts. I encourage them to continue doing what is healthy for the addict and to let go of what is unhealthy. "Do you love him enough," I ask, "to let him suffer the consequences of his actions, even if it involves something drastic like going to jail?"

Family and friends are usually caught between a rock and a hard place with regard to how to care for an addict. I commend them for their desire and commitment to help. But I encourage them to focus on their own well-being and the well-being of others who may need them just as much as the addict.

Parents may be so caught up in the fact that their teenage son has been using drugs that they neglect the needs of their pre-teen daughter. They need to minimize the attention given to the addict and avoid enabling him.

Most people are confused about what enabling means. Moms ask, "Does that mean I should just watch my daughter destroy her life? I shouldn't allow her to come home to shower and eat? Should I not pick her up from a drug house when she calls?"

Wives question, "Should I stop sleeping with my husband because I don't know where he's been? You seem to be telling me to not love him. Do you understand how difficult it is not to take care of his needs?"

It is difficult to tell an addicted loved one that you cannot help her without feeling tremendous guilt. But the question is not, "Do I help?" It should be, "Is what I am doing helping or hurting?"

Addicts know that internal struggles exist within the family, and they play the situation for all it's worth. They enjoy the attention their behavior generates. Negative attention is better than no attention at all. Many addicts relish the fact that family members are working hard to try to fix their problems. As long as they have the comforts of life—a place to sleep, food on the table, clean clothes, money in their pocket, and the attention of everyone in their immediate circle—what is their incentive to change?

If you are watching someone close to you succumb to an addiction, realize that you cannot control his addictive behavior. Once addiction is formed on an emotional level, the addict's primary responsibility is to build a strong defense to protect himself from attack.

Addicts know that family members will be disappointed in them, friends will reject their lifestyle, and the law may be out to get them. So they learn to lie, deceive, and cover up. It is important for you to be on the defense against manipulation. The addict wants sympathy, permission, acknowledgment, and anything else that will allow him to continue his behavior. You need to be strong in the face of this.

Misty was a twenty-five-year-old who married her twenty-eight-year-old college sweetheart, Perry. They were married for four years and had two children. Misty came to me complaining that Perry did not come home most evenings until almost midnight, claiming that his boss had issues with his job performance. "I know he's having an affair with an old girlfriend who moved into town six months ago."

I asked her to describe his behavior. She said that for the past six months Perry had been sneaking into the closet to take calls and whispering into the phone. When she confronted him, he said the calls had to do with a company legal issue and that he was getting ready to participate in a huge settlement he couldn't talk about.

Misty also mentioned that her husband had started getting loud and aggressive whenever they argued. His pager went off regularly and he no longer wore his wedding ring.

I asked her if Perry drank alcohol. She replied no. I asked if she thought he might be using drugs. Her response to that was even stronger. She was still convinced he was fooling around with an ex-girlfriend.

I explained to Misty that when people start practicing sneaky behavior, guard their privacy, lie, perform poorly at work, overreact to misunderstandings, and "lose" their jewelry, an affair might be the reason, but more likely, they are using drugs.

She left my office upset. But soon after our conversation she took a day off and followed him when he left work. To her surprise, he drove straight to a house that was known around town for providing drugs to people.

Anyone of any age, race, intelligence level, income, or status can get hooked on drugs. He doesn't even need to have money or a steady job. Addicts who don't have the financial resources find friends who will provide drugs as a gift or in exchange for some services such as sexual favors.

Thousands of groups and programs are available to deal with these problems. Mothers Against Drunk Drivers, Alcoholics Anonymous, Narcotics Anonymous, Cocaine Anonymous, Marijuana Anonymous, and Codependents Anonymous are just a few. Chemical dependency groups, inpatient hospitalization programs, and outpatient programs exist across the country. Insurance companies pay billions of dollars to treat addictive illnesses.

Who can count the number of deaths, murders, and suicides that have occurred as a result of substance abuse? How do you begin to measure the broken hearts, broken relationships, and broken promises encountered as a result of addictive behaviors?

Clara was married for twelve years to a husband who was addicted to sex. She came to my office saying, "I've had enough. I've stood by my husband even though he's been having an affair for nine years. I thought he just had a higher sex drive than I do. I figured he looked at porn videos and magazines because he was sexually dissatisfied with me. Then he started going to adult houses. I still made excuses because he wasn't involved with another woman. But later, he talked me into participating in multiple-partner sex. I went along with his request because at least he wasn't going out and doing it behind my back. Now, he wants my permission to have other sex partners without me. He justifies this sick request by pointing out that Old Testament men had multiple wives."

"Even though that was a cultural practice," I explained to Clara, "it wasn't a biblical one." I added that Exodus 20:14 clearly states, "You shall not commit adultery." In the New Testament, 1 Corinthians 6:9–10 says, "Do not be deceived; neither fornicators, nor idolaters, nor adulterers, nor effeminate, nor homosexuals, nor thieves, nor the covetous, nor drunkards, nor revilers, nor swindlers, will inherit the kingdom of God." Biblical truth always takes precedence over cultural practices.

I instructed Clara to stop obliging her husband and start suggesting that he seek therapy to deal with his addiction. She also needed to learn how to set healthy behavioral boundaries. I encouraged her to be firm in her decision not to participate in sinful activities with him, but also to be patient, encouraging, and compassionate with him regarding his struggle.

Clara and her husband are now both in counseling, and they are making slow but steady progress toward a healthy relationship.

Steve, a forty-four-year-old software expert for a major corporation and a strong deacon in an affluent church, was married for twenty years and had three children. He showed up in my office after his wife, Tanya, left with their fifteen-year-old twin sons. He said, "My wife thinks I have a drug problem, but I don't. She's just a controlling woman who wants to decide what friends I should have, what food I should eat, even the clothes I should wear."

"So, why are you in my office?" I asked him.

"I don't want to lose my sons," he answered tearfully.

I commended him for seeking help. As the session progressed, Steve revealed that he had started using marijuana in high school. When he got to college, pot no longer had the effect it used to. Someone at a party introduced him to cocaine and for the past twenty-five years, he had been using crack off and on.

Steve rationalized his problem because he had successfully maintained his job. He said there were so many company executives who did the same thing, it wasn't a big deal. Steve rarely went to dealers to buy drugs because he and his friends were affluent enough to have it delivered to them. They would meet at someone's house, watch television, and have cocaine parties.

His friends' wives sometimes joined them, and Steve didn't understand why Tanya wouldn't participate. "She and I used to smoke a few joints in college," he said, "but she stopped when she started going to church." He blamed Tanya for not understanding him. His father had used marijuana for years, and his mother never complained.

Tanya, who was at the session, said that their boys had started to question why their father was coming home so late. When they found drug paraphernalia while cleaning out their dad's car, they put two and two together and asked Tanya to be honest about what she knew about their father.

After hearing a message on 2 Timothy 2, Tanya decided to separate from Steve and to candidly share with the children what was going on.

After several sessions, I was able to convince Steve to realize that there is no such thing as a sophisticated, occasional drug user. Unfortunately, he was unable to control his habit.

Tanya thought long and hard about her next move. Ultimately, she decided to leave Steve and took the kids with her. She decided she would rather raise them alone than in a household where they would be exposed to drugs.

OVERCOMING ADDICTION

There are three key steps to claiming victory over an addiction.

Meditate on the Things of God

Romans 6:6 says that we are no longer slaves to sin. Since we are crucified with Christ, we are dead to sin. Though sin no longer reigns over us, we can still willingly place ourselves under its slavery. Even believers can choose to temporarily place themselves under sin's control, like a prisoner who has been set free but then decides to go back and live in the prison again. Why would someone do that? Because being behind bars brings comfort. It's what the prisoner knows. He doesn't have to step out of his comfort zone and overcome prejudices. By staying in prison, he gets three meals a day and plenty of exercise.

This may sound absurd, but we do the same thing when we decide to enslave ourselves to a particular sin. We love the feeling of our sin. We are satisfied with the bondage of it when we could have freedom in Christ. We would rather eat from the garbage dump than at the King's table! The enemy tells us we will be happier succumbing to sin than obeying God. But in reality, sin brings only fleeting pleasures that soon turn into pain and sorrow. Only the pleasures of God are eternal and completely satisfying.

The battleground is the mind. The mind informs the heart. Anything that is contrary to the Word of God should not be in our minds.

Human beings are prone to drift away from God rather than toward Him. So, how can we keep our minds pure? Second Corinthians 10:5 says, "We are destroying speculations and every lofty thing raised up against the knowledge of God, and we are taking every thought captive to the obedience of Christ." We need to build walls around our minds and guard what we let in them. We must compare any thoughts that enter our minds to God's righteous standard described in His Word.

Satan tries to tempt us by planting thoughts in our minds. What we do with those thoughts determines whether or not we have sinned. Temptation turns into sin when we harbor it in our hearts. Proverbs 4:23 says, "Watch over your heart with all diligence, for from it flow the springs of life."

While the mind is where temptation first arrives in the form of a thought, the heart is where sin takes root. That is why the heart must be guarded.

In the Bible the heart is considered the center of a person's being. That is where we must concentrate our efforts. "And do not be conformed to this world, but be transformed by the renewing of your mind" (Romans 12:2).

Some people say we should listen to our hearts. But the heart can be deceptive (Jeremiah 17:9). Proverbs 28:26 says, "He who trusts in his own heart is a fool, but he who walks wisely will be delivered."

The only way we can renew the mind is by bathing it in Scripture. In Hebrews 4:12 the Word of God is compared to a two-edged sword that can pierce or penetrate our souls. It is "able to judge the thoughts and intentions of the heart." The thoughts of man can be dangerous. We need to let them be judged by God's Word.

When an addictive thought comes into your mind, you can combat it with Scripture. God's Word is sufficient for all our needs and is powerful enough to keep us strong in the midst of temptation.

"In reference to your former manner of life, you lay aside the old self, which is being corrupted in accordance with the lusts of deceit, and that you be renewed in the spirit of your mind, and put on the new self, which in the likeness of God has been created in righteousness and holiness of the truth" (Ephesians 4:22–24). In Christ we have been made complete (Colossians 2:10) and we have been given every spiritual resource "pertaining to life and godliness, through the true knowledge of Him" by His divine power (2 Peter 1:3). We need to steadfastly cling to this powerful statement.

Colossians 3:1 says, "If you have been raised up with Christ, keep seeking the things above, where Christ is, seated at the right hand of God." The Greek word for "seek" means to earnestly desire or to zealously search after. It is more than a halfhearted appeal to stumble across the things of God; rather, it is to be on a zealous quest for the life-changing truths of God's Word. When we begin to earnestly desire these things, we will find the attraction of sin begin to wane.

Resist the Power of Sin

We may believe that sin is so powerful it can force us to obey it, but that is not the case. James 1:14 says that "each one is tempted when he is carried away and enticed by his own lust." The only person we can blame is ourselves. Satan may tempt us, but we choose whether or not to follow his suggestions. There is no temptation too big to overcome.

Rely on the Power of the Holy Spirit

Paul said in Romans 7:22–23, "For I joyfully concur with the law of God in the inner man, but I see a different law in the members of my body, waging war against the law of my mind and making me a prisoner of the law of sin which is in my members." Paul saw a fierce war being waged in his body. If he had stopped at this verse, the battle would seem hopeless. But he went on to say, "Wretched man that I am! Who will set me free from the body of this death?" (verse 24). He answered his own question by saying, "Thanks be to God through Jesus Christ our Lord!" (verse 25). The answer to being saved from our slavery to sin is Jesus Christ.

The Holy Spirit empowers us to turn away from addictions. A person suffering from addiction may believe he is helpless to overcome his destructive habit. But God calls us to take all of our anxious thoughts to Him. When we believe we need something other than God, we are caught up in a lie of the devil. We are not slaves to anything.

This freedom does not come from our own discipline. In 2 Timothy 1:7 we are told, "For God has not given us a spirit of timidity, but of power and love and discipline."

Take Responsibility for Your Actions

We are a society of blamers. We always look for a "scapegoat" to blame for our moral failures. Though events in our past may have had a great effect on our present, they did not *make* us sin. If a person was sexually abused as a child, for example, that incident will affect many areas of that person's adult life. But if the abused person abuses someone else, she cannot blame the person who abused her. We are all responsible for our own actions.

HOW TO COPE

When someone you love is addicted, you must exercise four qualities.

Patience

It takes time for a person to overcome addiction. Habits do not form overnight; neither will a cure. We are to be gentle and patient toward one who has sinned, without compromising God's standard or jeopardizing the sinner's overall well-being. Tough love appears harsh, but in actuality, you are helping a person develop himself emotionally and spiritually. You are not letting him off the hook when he puts himself at risk. If there are no consequences to his actions, he will almost certainly repeat the action.

Understanding

Someone who has an addiction needs understanding, not a list of dos and don'ts. Romans 8:1 says, "Therefore there is now no condemnation for those who are in Christ Jesus." We must be compassionate toward someone who is addicted. We can let him know that his sin is unacceptable, but we are not to look down upon him with a self-righteous attitude. We all battle our own strongholds.

Grace

Christians are saved by grace. Ephesians 2:8 says, "For by grace you have been saved through faith." We are also to walk in grace. Ephesians 2:10 says, "For we are His workmanship, created in Christ Jesus for good works, which God prepared beforehand so that we would walk in them." Using appropriate Scriptures, we should point a person who is addicted to the grace of God.

Mercy and Forgiveness

Addicted persons often behave irrationally. Though we are never to condone such behavior, we are to have mercy on sinners. Jude 22–23 says, "And have mercy on some, who are doubting; save others, snatching them out of the fire; and on some have mercy with fear, hating even the garment polluted by the flesh." While this verse tells us to hate the sin, we must not hate the person who sins. Even when someone displays addictive behaviors, she is still loved by God. Romans 5:1 says we are justified by faith, not by the works that we do.

HELP IS AVAILABLE

It is difficult to recover from addiction without help from one-on-one counseling or support groups. Fortunately, help is available.

Through the Local Church

Many churches have support groups to help addicts overcome their addictive behavior. Some have twelve-step programs developed by church professionals. There may also be support groups to help struggling and frustrated family members who are not sure how to deal with the crisis.

The church's main goal should be to help the individual spiritually, through encouraging a higher level of commitment to Christ.

However, a person's unwillingness to do this should not deter the church from helping.

The addict may need to be referred to a local rehabilitation center.

We should avoid preaching and lecturing to the addict. These people need help, not condemnation.

Following are a few guidelines:

- Encourage the addict to attend a Bible study and join a Bible-teaching church.

- Advise the addict to cease communication with any friends who might pressure him to continue in his addiction—even if that means moving to another neighborhood.

- Support the addict through prayer, asking God to help her develop the courage to make good decisions.

Through Your Community

Some physicians specialize in treating addictive behavior. Professional drug abuse counselors are trained to deal with drug issues. Regardless of where you live, help is just a phone call away.

If you have even the slightest feeling that you might be addicted, let me encourage you to get help. Contact your pastor, friend, family member, doctor, or a treatment center in your area. Accept that you have a problem, you are powerless over it, and you need someone to help you.

If you continue in your addiction, you will end up paying a heavy price, whether it be losing your house, your job, your spouse, your children, or any number of other things that add quality and meaning to your existence. However, with the proper help, you can overcome your addiction and live a happy, healthy, and productive life.

SUMMARY POINTS

✓ Addiction is a form of bondage to an impulsive, habitual behavior that has taken root in a person's life. One can be addicted to drugs, alcohol, sex, cigarettes, shopping, work, gambling, food, and television, to name a few.

✓ Families play a crucial role in establishing the habits and values that a child will adopt later in life. We must be sure that our actions, not just our words, are sending the correct messages to our children.

✓ Addicts usually realize the effect their condition has on others. On the one hand, they feel guilty and ashamed by it; on the other hand, they subconsciously enjoy the attention it draws to them.

✓ If someone is displaying odd behavior, we shouldn't assume we know the source of the problem. We must seek input from others. We may have to show tough love with a caring and godly spirit.

✓ It is vital that we meditate upon the things of God and keep our thoughts focused on His Word in order to guard our hearts against the temptations of the world. We must rely on our renewed minds to point us in the right direction.

✓ We can trust the Holy Spirit's power. Alone, we can do nothing, but 2 Timothy 1:7 makes it clear that we are well equipped to overcome adversity through God's power.

QUESTIONS TO PONDER

✓ What might I be addicted to? Why do I choose this person, activity, or object for comfort?

✓ Am I the type of person who avoids pain at all costs? Am I willing to let myself be uncomfortable in order to grow?

✓ Am I enabling someone who is addicted because I am fearful of what may happen if I don't rescue him? Am I assisting out of love or guilt? How might I be contributing to that person's demise?

✓ Do I regularly meditate on God's Word? Can I recall appropriate Scriptures in time of need? Am I aware of the Holy Spirit's power and sufficiency during trying times?

✓ According to James 1:14–15, can Satan "make" me sin? Why or why not?

7

If you *only* knew...
<u>My Depression</u>

The subject of depression causes a lot of confusion and division among Christians. I've been on several radio programs where the topic was discussed and people called in with various opposing views. Some stated a belief that depression is merely a state of mind that everyone experiences at some point. Others argued that it is a serious illness that requires intervention.

Still others say Christians don't get depressed. We feel guilty and sad because of our sin, but if we stop sinning, we will be all right. These people believe there is no need for counseling or medication for depression.

Conflicting views about mental health and God's ability to heal us in that area have many Christians at odds. Since there is so much controversy surrounding the topic, a person who suffers from depression may not be feel comfortable seeking help.

Additionally, mental ailments are not as cut-and-dried as physical problems. So healing is not as easily measured.

There is also a stigma to having less than optimal mental health. The average person does not distinguish between someone who has a mental disorder and someone who is mentally ill or mentally challenged. A person who is physically limited is called *disabled;* a person who struggles with mental or emotional issues is called *crazy.*

All of these factors combine to make the topic of mental health sensitive, controversial, and secretive.

Years ago, I thought that Christians who claimed to be depressed simply didn't have enough faith in God. But after an in-depth study on the subject, conducted with an open mind, I began to realize how wrong I was.

Based on my studies and experience as a counselor, I believe depression is a serious emotional condition that born-again Christians can and do feel. Many people suffer from undiagnosed depression that is explained away with such platitudes as "She needs to be filled more with the Spirit" or "Depression is a sign of weakness."

Some church leaders, who are not clinically trained, may be so afraid of their parishioners getting counseling from non-Christian psychologists that they actually discourage those who look to them for advice from getting the help they need.

A few pastors actually make fun of people with emotional conditions such as depression. They may even encourage those who are on medication to do away with their medicines. In an attempt to prove that God can do all things and heal all diseases, these church leaders are jeopardizing the mental health of their congregation. Luke, the gospel writer, was a physician, and he believed strongly in the Lord's ability to heal directly. Yet he also recognized God's ability to heal indirectly, through others.

MYTHS ABOUT DEPRESSION

A myth is a false perception about a subject based on a person's cultural background, upbringing, and/or society. With this in mind, let's examine some of the myths surrounding the psychology of depression.

The Racial Myth

I've heard people state that depression is a white person's problem because only they have the money and time to be depressed, or that white people are the only ones who have really deep issues. After all, they argue, how many psychologists, counselors, or psychiatrists are there in Africa? But just because a condition isn't diagnosed, that doesn't mean it is nonexistent.

I believe thousands of people in third-world countries (as well as underprivileged areas of the United States) suffer from depression just as they suffer from other illnesses. Due to a lack of resources, diagnosis and treatment are usually not possible.

The Modern Myth

A pastor friend told me he thought the subject of depression has been blown out of proportion in recent times. "Fifty years ago," he said, "most people in this country didn't have jobs with insurance benefits to cover the cost of professional counseling. They laid their problems on the altar and lived longer lives."

I pointed out to my friend that a lot of people in the previous generation drank too much. Sad, hopeless, and helpless, with no end in sight, they numbed their pain with alcohol so they could forget their depression for a while. A lot of those people died of alcoholism.

The Religion Myth

I once heard a television preacher refer to counselors as "agents of the devil" coming into the church to snatch and destroy the people of God. I'm sure he was attempting to protect his flock from being deceived by some non-Christian psychologists who had their own agendas that didn't include wholeness for their clients. But it would have served a greater purpose had he explained his concern in detail instead of making a sweeping statement.

Living in sin can create guilt, sadness, and anxiety for a Christian, which may contribute to feelings of depression. However, just because you feel guilty and sad about sin, that doesn't mean you are depressed.

I have talked with church leaders who have different opinions about depression. Some say it is simply a guilt feeling brought on by living a disobedient life. They believe that seeking help for an emotional problem is a sign of a lack of maturity in Christ.

Unfortunately, most pastors are not trained to recognize the symptoms of depression.

The Gender Myth

Both men and women are capable of feeling negative emotions. Typically, however, men don't respond well to emotional problems. Most of them are brought up to believe that expressing feelings is a sign of weakness. They may need to be encouraged to open up about their emotional well-being and to seek proper diagnosis from qualified professionals.

TYPES OF COUNSELING

Let's say a Christian couple wants a divorce simply because they no longer love each other. They make appointments with three different types of counselors.

The *nouthetic counselor* uses only Scripture as a frame of reference. He considers this couple's desire for a divorce sinful. He will quote Bible verses that prove God does not approve of divorce in their case.

The *secular counselor* applies only psychological theory. She finds out why the marriage is not working and offers different perspectives designed to resolve the conflict. If, after several visits, the issues are not resolved, she may decide that the next step is whatever the individuals want, even if that is to dissolve the relationship.

The *biblical integrationist* applies secular techniques along with scriptural recommendations. If he suspects one of the spouses may be in physical danger from abuse, he may encourage separation until the abuser obtains help. However, unless there is evidence of unrepentant sexual immorality, this counselor will encourage the couple not to pursue a divorce.

To some pastors, any practice other than nouthetic counseling is non-Christian. To others, the integration approach qualifies as Christian counseling.

The problem with nouthetic counseling is that not all emotional problems are caused by sin. Depression may be caused by circumstances or physical problems. Secular counseling falls short because any approach that doesn't include God and His Word is incomplete and cannot, therefore, bring wholeness. I believe that integration is the most complete approach to treatment.

WHY DON'T PEOPLE SEEK HELP?

There are many reasons people don't try to get help for depression.

Access

One common reason is that a person does not have convenient access to a mental health provider. He may live in a rural area, or even a major city that is far from a concentration of therapists. There might be counselors in nearly every city and town in America, but finding a good one may be difficult.

Many people have to rely on friends, or the bus, or their own two feet to get them around. If such a person needs to see a professional about her problems, it may be difficult for her to overcome the obstacle of how to get there.

Cost

Another common limitation is insufficient or nonexistent health care benefits. Companies are increasingly unwilling to pay for nonphysical health issues.

Some churches and a few colleges offer lower-cost counseling services. In addition, several books have been written by respected psychologists and counselors for the benefit of those who are suffering from depression.

Embarrassment

Some people hesitate to see a therapist because they feel it would be embarrassing to run into someone they know at the office. Ironically, they don't seem to consider the fact that the other person is also getting counseling, so there would be no reason for him to pass judgment.

Social Boundaries

Sometimes, the people I counsel become uncomfortable when they see me at church. While I would never betray the confidence of a counseling session, some clients are nervous about socializing with someone who knows so much about their personal issues.

Belief Systems

Comedian Steve Harvey once played a TV dad whose family tried to convince him to go to therapy. He refused, saying, "I'll keep my feelings bottled up inside until they harden and become a physical problem. Then I'll go see a real doctor." Steve Harvey's character let his personal misconceptions become a hindrance to getting proper mental health treatment. He didn't believe psychologists were legitimate doctors, probably because he didn't think that mental or emotional issues were valid problems that needed to be addressed by a professional.

Projection

It is common for people to make the assessment that "other people" need therapy—those who are poor, unstable, of another race, with a different background or socio-economic class, etc.

Denial

Sometimes the biggest obstacle to getting help is simply recognizing that you or a family member, friend, or church member has a mental condition that needs attention.

All of the above hesitations are normal human reactions, and there is nothing wrong with most of them. However, if a person does not move beyond these stages, his condition will remain unaddressed and, therefore, unresolved. He will continue feeling hopeless, helpless, and/or worthless.

IDENTIFYING EMOTIONAL ILLNESSES

In order to understand which approach will best assist with recovery and/or management of an emotional illness, it is necessary to identify the type of illness a person is suffering from.

Clinical Depression

Myra had been feeling hopeless for months. She attended church every Sunday and Wednesday, read her Bible daily, prayed without ceasing, listened to her pastor's tapes, and spent time with her boyfriend, but nothing gave her hope. She participated in yoga, mentored a child, and took a creative writing class. Though these activities were interesting and fulfilling, Myra didn't really enjoy any of them.

Even her job didn't satisfy her. Myra was an occupational therapist who originally chose the field because she wanted to help people. But over the years she became more annoyed with her patients than inspired and uplifted by them. When she came home from work, all she wanted to do was sleep. She lacked energy and had difficulty eating. She dropped a full clothes size and was on her way to losing another.

Myra cried frequently, then felt guilty for crying. *There are much worse things I could be going through,* she thought. *Why am I so unhappy?* She didn't want to kill herself but thought she'd be relieved if God would just take her life because the world would be better off without her. Sometimes she felt like running away.

Friends told her to pray more, have more faith, and confess all known sins. She followed their advice, but nothing seemed to help.

Finally Myra's father encouraged her to see a counselor. She felt ashamed about talking to a professional because she had always thought that only emotionally weak people sought psychological help. However, to please her father, Myra made an appointment.

After two sessions the counselor told Myra she had a clinical depression. Medication was prescribed to help manage her imbalance, and she continued seeing the counselor on a regular basis.

Two years later, Myra is now well-adjusted, emotionally healthy, and living a joy-filled life.

Panic Disorder

Andrea was a go-getter. As the assistant principal of a private high school, she had tremendous responsibilities and performed her job well. She loved her work and approached all tasks with an attitude of excellence. Some of her colleagues considered her a perfectionist.

Despite her fulfilling life, Andrea began feeling anxious and sad. One day, while driving to work, a car pulled close to hers, making her feel as though she would lose control of the vehicle. Several minutes after the incident, she was still unable to calm down.

A few days later, during a meeting with the principal, she suffered the same kind of emotions, fearing that she might lose her job and worrying that her husband would leave her.

As these unfounded reactions started occurring more frequently, Andrea tried to reduce stress by working out, taking vitamin supplements, and getting regular massages. She jogged six days a week and ate only organic foods from the local market. She spent hours on the Internet getting the latest information on health and fitness. Yet she felt increasingly worried and anxious.

One day at school, she blew up at a student. One of her coworkers witnessed the incident. He pulled her aside and told her he'd been observing her behavior. He recommended she see a psychiatrist.

On her first visit, Andrea learned that she had a condition known as panic disorder. The psychiatrist prescribed antidepressant medications and saw Andrea on a regular basis. After just a few weeks, she was able to start leading a normal life.

Schizophrenia

Robert lived in a very small town. Every day he wore a sweater, a tattered overcoat, and huge boots, even in eighty-degree weather. The townspeople smiled at him when they walked by and he greeted them warmly in return. On Sundays Robert went to church and sat quietly in the back pew. He went to convenience stores at mealtimes and asked for food. He never paid, but the shopkeepers didn't seem to mind. Children laughed at him, but older people said, "Leave him alone. He's not bothering anybody."

Sometimes Robert sat by himself at the park, shouting comments about the state of the nation. He seemed to be talking to someone no one else could see.

One day Robert fell and broke his leg. He was hospitalized in the city, where no one knew him. A psychiatrist diagnosed him as having schizophrenia.

The psychiatrist put Robert on medication and sent him back home. Though he still occasionally suffers bouts of irrational behavior, he is able to function normally within society. He got a job removing trash, and he is staying at a homeless shelter until he can find permanent housing.

CAUSES AND TYPES OF DEPRESSION

There are numerous reasons people become depressed and various kinds of depression. It is important to properly diagnose the type and source of depression in order to determine the appropriate method of treatment.

Situational Depression

This form of depression is caused by ignored stressors in one's environment. It is typified by a sadness that lingers for months at a time. Sadness itself is not depression, but the inability to process and eliminate the source of sadness over time is.

We all grow up with certain expectations in life. Some women look forward to getting married and having two children, a dog or a cat, a nice car, and a 2500-square-foot home by age thirty-two.

When they reach forty and are still living in a one-room apartment without a husband, child, or pet, if there are no mechanisms in place to handle feelings of disappointment over their situation, they may become depressed.

Several years ago, I counseled a thirty-eight-year-old woman with those typical expectations. "I've attended church faithfully all my life," she said, "and I haven't done anything immoral. But," she added with tears in her eyes, "I'm almost forty years old, I'm not married, and I don't have any children."

Attempting to encourage herself about her situation, she said, "I'm not going to get depressed over it. If I'm still unmarried when I turn thirty-nine, I'll just get pregnant, have a child, and find the man later."

Most men expect, by age thirty-five, to have a great job that pays six figures, be in a management position, drive a Lexus, Mercedes, or Cadillac, own a 3000-square-foot home in a nice neighborhood, be married to a beautiful woman, have a few children, and be a member of the local country club. When reality hits that he is forty-one, has been divorced twice, has one child he is not raising, lives in a studio apartment, and works the graveyard shift making ten dollars an hour, he can become depressed about his situation.

The inability to process what is happening through positive filters or to lift oneself up—a skill that can be acquired through a strong biblical belief system—can push one into depression.

Additionally, unresolved issues stemming from childhood abuse (sexual, emotional, or physical) can lead to depression as an adult. Television shows remind these victims of childhood sorrow, and relationships with a significant other may bring up unpleasant situations.

Becky, a thirty-two-year-old woman I counseled, had a major depressive disorder. She was angry with her mother, so I asked her to write a letter to help her let go of her feelings. Her letter said, in essence:

> Mom,
> I want to start by saying that I love you, which is what I have been praying to be able to do. Through therapy, I am learning to forgive you and move

on. I know you blame me for ruining your life. But the truth is, you ruined mine.

I don't understand why you didn't believe me when I told you, at age ten, that your husband was messing with me when I was asleep. At twelve, when I told you he was having intercourse with me, why did you believe him over me? When you caught him having sex with me, I thought for sure you would finally leave him or put him out, but you didn't. Why did you stay with him and allow him to sleep with both of us?

I had to go to the school nurse to get birth control pills so I wouldn't get pregnant by your husband. The nurse asked me to tell her what was going on at home. She promised she wouldn't tell anyone. I begged her to get me some help since you refused to protect me.

When she called Child Protective Services and they took me to a foster home, why didn't you come to visit? Why did you hate me?

When my father got custody of me, even though he was an alcoholic, why didn't you at least call to see how I was doing? When I told you my dad's friends were touching me sexually, why didn't you rescue me?

When I got pregnant by one of Dad's friends and I had to leave his house, I was homeless for a long while, but you didn't care about what happened to me or your grandchild.

It has been twenty years since I saw you, and you still don't want a relationship with me. Why? I cry every time my friends talk about their mothers because I don't really have one.

After writing the letter, Becky decided not to send it. She felt so relieved just to evaluate what had happened to her, she began taking further steps toward healing.

Many young couples become deeply depressed soon after the wedding. Most go into marriage believing every promise they made to each other while dating. Newlywed couples often come into my office saying things like, "He told me he would never go to bed angry with me, and now he can easily go a week without even speaking to me." Or, "She promised she would never use sex to control me, but she is completely unresponsive to my advances just because she's angry about something I said three days ago."

Most promises made during dating are spoken with honest intentions, but the emotional high that controls us during courtship simply is not present in marriage. Sadly, some people, even Christians, can deceive others or misrepresent the truth.

Biological Depression

In June 2001 Andrea Yates, a thirty-seven-year-old mother, was sentenced to life in prison for drowning her five children. According to her physician, Mrs. Yates was overwhelmed by the growth of her family, had extreme levels of shame and guilt about her thoughts of harming her children, and entertained irrational ideas of the consequences of harming them.

George and Tina brought their fourteen-year-old daughter, Lisa, to my office, concerned about a suicide note she had written to her friends in school. After talking with Lisa's parents, I discovered that Tina had an anxiety condition that had not been diagnosed. George suffered from depression.

Lisa described her symptoms, which included fleeting thoughts of extreme anger, fear that nobody liked her, and feelings of worthlessness that went beyond normal teenage angst. She found these emotions nearly impossible to control. Tina mentioned that she had gone through similar experiences as an adolescent. I concluded that Lisa's depression was biological in nature.

Some forms of depression run in the family. Medical physicians ask patients to provide a history of illness in their families. A good counselor needs the same type of information. Family history can help distinguish between biological and situational depression.

A patient's ability to recover without medication is another indicator.

OVERCOMING DEPRESSION

Although it may take time, depression can be overcome. The length of the road to recovery will be based on whether the depression is situational or biological, and on the individual's willingness and ability to work hard in treatment.

Situational Depression

Usually, if the causes of depression are eliminated or perceived differently, the condition goes away. Sometimes all the individual needs is someone who will listen, encourage, or offer some options that the individual may not have considered. With most cases of situational depression, empathy is all that's required.

About nine years ago, a six-foot-eight, 300-pound fellow named Kurt walked into my office. I began our meeting in prayer, then asked why he was visiting me. He immediately broke down in tears. He had been married for sixteen years and had two lovely children: a fourteen-year-old daughter and a twelve-year-old son. But he had been having problems with his wife for two years. Three days before our visit, Kurt was served with divorce papers.

For thirty minutes all I did was listen. Occasionally, when his legs were crossed, I reached out and placed my hand on his shoe to comfort him.

That was all the big guy needed. He went home that night and told his wife, "Dr. Acho squeezed my toes. What a terrific counselor!"

Kurt's outlook concerning his situation changed. He stopped feeling sorry for himself and recognized God's control of his life. His wife told him he was finally what she had been looking for—a positive, strong husband. She called my office and made an appointment. After counseling, she withdrew the divorce, they reconciled, and today they are a happy couple.

I recently received a call from a church member named Floyd who, six years prior, married a non-Christian woman. She eventually gave her life to Christ. Despite that, they had marital problems for almost five years. One day, Floyd came home from work and found the house empty because his wife had left him. When he called her, she said, "The marriage is over. From now on, our communication will be through the attorneys."

I spent forty minutes listening to Floyd and letting him vent. He knew I could not get his wife to change her mind. But just by being there for him, I was able to help him process his feelings and minimize his anxiety over the situation.

We live in a society where family standards have broken down and people are either too busy or too selfish to invest time in one another. Sometimes all someone needs is for a brother or sister to commit to caring, listening, and walking with him.

In many situations, lay counseling can be every bit as effective as psychiatric help. If desired, a professional can be consulted to evaluate the situation and support the effectiveness of the lay counseling.

Biological Depression

People with serious mental conditions (such as multiple personality disorder, obsessive compulsive disorder, bipolar disorder, or schizophrenia) should be seen by a psychiatrist who can provide medication therapy. They must commit to years of treatment because such emotional problems don't go away quickly.

All psychiatric disorders have biological, psychosocial, and genetic components. When symptoms cause clinically significant distress or impairment in functioning, and the individual is unresponsive to social support and help from nonprofessionals, it is time to investigate medication therapy. Medicine usually works best when there are physical symptoms such as noticeable changes in weight, appetite, sleep patterns, energy levels, and/or psychomotor retardation and agitation (thinking and moving slowly or quickly).

Inconsistent treatment only works to the detriment of the patient. People sometimes come to me and say they have been going to a counselor for two years but are frustrated because they don't seem to be getting better. When I ask them how many times they went the first year, the average response is about five. With problems that are biological in nature, five to ten visits in two years may not produce tangible results.

WHAT CAN WE DO?

If you suspect that someone you know may be suffering from depression, I encourage you to be bold enough to say to them, "I've noticed some things happening with you, and I'm concerned. Would you consider talking to a counselor to evaluate what's going on?"

If you notice a close friend or family member, Christian or unbeliever, exhibiting abnormal behavior or expressing irrational ideas about harming someone, immediately suggest that person see a counselor. If she agrees to go, help her evaluate the different options by finding local churches or organizations that offer counseling programs. Encourage her to call them, then step back and let her handle things from there. She needs to take some steps on her own, and her desire to improve has to come from her heart.

If your friend or family member rejects the idea of counseling, you have two options.

1. If he is suicidal or at risk of causing harm to others, you need to intervene immediately. Contact an authority figure (pastor, police officer, social worker) who can step in. Do not try to tackle this matter on your own. Qualified professionals deal with emergency situations like this regularly. Let them help.

2. If he is emotionally stable and unlikely to cause harm, you need to come to terms with the fact that he has rejected help. Pray that God will touch his heart so he can reach out to someone for healing. Allow the Holy Spirit to work in his life, and be available if he changes his mind.

SUMMARY POINTS

✓ Depression falls into two categories:

⇨ Situational depression can be brought on by a single event or a series of events, or false expectations. If the sufferer has not learned to process and eliminate the source of sadness, she may become depressed. She should seek help through a trusted professional or lay counselor.

⇨ Biological depression has genetic origins. The sufferer can usually point to a family history of mental or emotional struggles. If this is the case, treatment must be administered by a psychiatrist trained in medication therapy.

✓ We should be willing to listen and provide comfort when others share their problems and concerns with us. It is important that we suggest someone get help if we observe any extreme thought patterns or behaviors.

QUESTIONS TO PONDER

✓ Do I have any preconceived notions about depression?

✓ Have I been told that I should be able to work through my problems without help from anyone?

✓ Has anyone suggested to me that if I were stronger in my faith, I wouldn't have thoughts of depression?

✓ Am I an optimist or a pessimist? Can I see solutions to my problems? If not, am I able to accept that all problems are temporary?

✓ Am I willing to step out of my comfort zone and get the help I need? If not, what is stopping me? Can I see ways around my obstacles?

✓ What is my family history of emotional struggles, depression, and mental health?

8

THERE IS HOPE

Is your current situation so bad that you wonder if God is in it? Do you believe you've blown it so badly that the Lord can never bless you? If you think there's no hope for you, you're wrong. No one has sinned so terribly that he can never again be a benefit to the kingdom of God. No circumstances are so horrible that God cannot use them for His glory. We are never at a place where we are totally useless to God. But if Satan can convince you that your life is beyond repair, he'll have you right where he wants you.

Erica was a single female with the desire to be married, have children, and own a house. She tried to live her life according to God's Word. However, she had premarital sex with her last boyfriend, John, but stopped once she made up her mind that she would wait until she was married, but he subsequently broke up with her. She tried to accept that God knew what was best for her, but as months went by, Erica began questioning her self-worth and womanhood. Her faith in God with regard to her dating life grew weak. She felt that God had let her down and believed she would never get married.

Erica sought counseling and finally accepted that she does have value. She learned that even if she never marries, God loves her. She realized there is still hope for her to be a wife and mother.

Hope is a word we use commonly. For example, we might say, "I hope I can go to the ball game tonight." This kind of hope always carries with it a note of uncertainty. We are unsure of whether or not we can attain what we want.

One of Webster's definitions of *hope* is "wishful trust."[1] In such a case, hope is simply a desire, like when we are urged to make a wish before blowing out the candles on our birthday cake.

But that is not the kind of hope found in God's Word.

THE NATURE OF HOPE

Hope, by itself, is not based on anything concrete. The crucial key lies in where our hope is placed. If we hope for a new car, but acquiring one depends on our ability to pay for it, our hope is placed on our income. And financial situations can change at any moment.

However, hope is also a biblical concept. Hebrews 11:1 says, "Faith is the assurance of things hoped for." In 1 Corinthians 13:7, we are told that love "hopes all things." We are called to have hope in God, the One who made the earth by His word.

How do we lose hope? How do we get to the point of saying that a marriage is no longer salvageable? How do we become so sick of our jobs that we no longer want to work there? When do we come to the point that we declare we will never forgive a person who has wronged us?

Hope disappears when we become shortsighted. We lose our ability to look beyond the present and see that good can come from our situation. We fail to see things the way God does. We see a couple who bickers constantly instead of a family the Lord is making into His image. We see a wife living in sin instead of a woman who was created to glorify Him. We take our eyes off what He is doing and focus on our circumstances.

Moses did the same thing. He was commissioned by God to rescue the Israelites from Egypt. What an incredible blessing! But Moses didn't look at it that way. He asked, "Who am I, that I should go to Pharaoh, and that I should bring the sons of Israel out of Egypt?" (Exodus 3:11). Moses was right—he was not the one to rescue the Israelites out of Egypt. God was. But Moses assumed that he was solely responsible to lead the Israelites. God assured him by saying, "Certainly I will be with you" (verse 12).

Moses still didn't get it. He asked what he should say if the Egyptians asked why God had sent him. God told him to say, "I AM has sent me to you" (verse 14).

Still Moses didn't comprehend. He asked, "What if they will not believe me? . . . For they may say, 'The Lord has not appeared to you.'" (4:1).

God, with awesome patience, gave Moses two miraculous signs to show that He was with him. But Moses still focused on his situation. He scrambled for an excuse not to act. He explained that he had never been eloquent.

God replied that He would be his mouth and give him the appropriate words to say. Moses responded, "Please, Lord, now send the message by whomever You will" (verse 13). He was asking God to send someone else to do the job.

The Lord became angry with Moses. Time and time again, He showed Moses how He was planning to deliver him, but he refused to listen. Moses couldn't see that he was fit to do what the Lord was asking of him.

Do you sometimes feel like Moses, not knowing why God is allowing the situation you are experiencing? The Lord is still in control. If He is allowing you to experience difficulties, instead of wondering if you have been cursed, place your hope in Him. Don't give up. God promises that all things will work together for good. (See Romans 8:28.)

Tony and Anne lived together for two years prior to their marriage. Two and a half years later, they began counseling. Anne was still dealing with issues from a previous marriage. She often became angry with Tony. But after a few sessions, she started making changes.

Once Anne began pleasing her husband, Tony started treating her with disrespect. Eventually Anne asked Tony to leave their home. When he had been away for about a month, he made an effort to talk to her about what had been going on between them. Anne agreed to let Tony back into the house, but neither of them established any ground rules. Their problems continued. Tony said things to Anne that were belittling and demeaning. Anne began having ulcers, migraine headaches, and hair loss.

After several months of denying her depression, Anne sought psychiatric help. She was told she needed to start taking anti-depressants.

Sadly, Anne did not believe that God could see her through her pain. Without hope that her situation could get better, she didn't see the point of going on. One day she took too many pills and died of an overdose.

We should never give up on God. We must allow Him time to work on our hearts and our situations to bring about change. Regardless of how bad things may look, He is still able to work miracles.

THE POWER OF GOD

Even when we see the incredible glory of God, we sometimes find it hard to trust Him. We realize that He created the material world with the breath of His mouth, yet we do not think He can create peace in our hearts. If He could save us when we were His enemies and give us peace with Him, why would we not believe that He can give us peace with our mates?

We are to have hope in the power of God at work in us. But Satan lies to us, telling us that God has dealt with our sin long enough, and this time, our sin has pushed us over the edge. The Lord no longer wants to deal with us. Satan tries to convince us that there is no hope.

Would you still rejoice in God if your business failed? Would you be joyful if you were unemployed and had no prospects for another job? This was Habakkuk's situation when he said he would still trust in the Lord. Habakkuk 3:17–19 reads:

> Though the fig tree should not blossom
> And there be no fruit on the vines,
> Though the yield of the olive should fail
> And the fields produce no food,
> Though the flock should be cut off from the fold
> And there be no cattle in the stalls,
> Yet I will exult in the Lord,
> I will rejoice in the God of my salvation.
> The Lord God is my strength,
> And He has made my feet like hinds' feet,
> And makes me walk on my high places.

Did Habakkuk question where God would get his provisions? No. He looked past his immediate circumstances and considered the Lord his ultimate "food." He realized that God was far above any circumstances he had. Habakkuk became encouraged by God's presence and found hope.

There should never be a time when a believer in Christ is without hope. God has promised that He will make us into the image of His Son. In Galatians 4:19 Paul said that he was "in labor" with the Galatian church until Christ would be formed in them. First Corinthians 3:7 says, "So then neither the one who plants nor the one who waters is anything, but God who causes the growth." We are to look forward to the assured hope of God transforming us into Christ's image.

Paul observed in 2 Corinthians 4:16, "Therefore we do not lose heart, but though our outer man is decaying, yet our inner man is being renewed day by day."

These verses all have one central theme: We are being made into Christ's likeness more each day.

God never sees situations as hopeless. He is in complete control of our circumstances, and if He hasn't lost hope in our situation, neither should we. Philippians 1:6 says, "For I am confident of this very thing, that He who began a good work in you will perfect it until the day of Christ Jesus."

If anyone should have been hopeless, it was Peter. He gave in to peer pressure and denied being a disciple. It would have been easy for Peter to say, "I've messed up so badly God can never use me again." But he didn't. He became even more dedicated to Christ.

Later, in John 21:15–17, the Lord challenged Peter's dedication by asking him if he loved Him. The word for love that Christ used here was *agape*. Agape love is profound, unconditional love. It shows the utmost commitment and complete devotion.

Peter replied that he loved Jesus, but he used a different word: *phileo*. Phileo love has a lesser degree and commitment than agape. Peter was too ashamed, after his past failure, to admit his full devotion to the Lord. He needed to learn a lesson on commitment.

Jesus came down to Peter's level and asked him again if he loved Him, but this time He used Peter's word, *phileo*. The Lord was questioning whether or not Peter could truly claim phileo love.

Then the Lord asked Peter if he loved Him "more than these." *These* referred to the other disciples. Jesus was demanding that Peter be fully devoted to Him.

At this point, Peter had a decision to make. He could wallow in his self-pity or learn from his past. Peter chose to grow stronger in God's grace.

In Acts 2:22–36, Peter stood up in the midst of a group of men in Jerusalem and delivered a strong message, witnessing for his Lord. At the end, he said, "Therefore, let all the house of Israel know for certain that God has made Him both Lord and Christ—this Jesus whom you crucified." About three thousand souls were saved that day (verse 41).

This is quite a turnaround for Peter. In the wake of great failure, he chose to focus on the One who was able to strengthen him.

When you begin to wonder why distressing things happen, remember there is always hope, no matter how bleak the situation looks. God is working in you. He will never leave you or give up on you. Jude 24 says that He is "able to keep you from stumbling, and to make you stand in the presence of His glory blameless with great joy."

SUMMARY POINTS

✓ Merely having hope is not enough. Our hope must be in God, the only One who can fulfill our needs and desires.

✓ There are several biblical examples of people who lost hope, as well as those who lost hope but regained it when they believed in God's ability to transform them through their circumstances.

✓ We must learn to see beyond the present. God is not constrained by what happened yesterday or what is happening today.

QUESTIONS TO PONDER

✓ Have I lost hope? Lack of hope is based on a situation or state of existence, both of which God is able to change.

✓ Am I practicing any behavior that is inhibiting my walk with the Lord? Is there something I am doing to help Satan make my situation look hopeless?

9

A WORD FOR PASTORS

As shepherds, we have an obligation to watch over God's flock. This does not mean just preaching on Sundays and conducting Bible study every Wednesday. Don't get me wrong; the preparation and delivery of a powerful message from God's Word is a major part of shepherding the flock. Church members need to be fed. However, some in the church body may be hungry but unable to eat because of a lack of appetite or some other condition. It is unproductive to force-feed someone who is too weak to take in nourishment.

If pastors are aware of the condition of their members, they can then train their congregation to look out for one another's well-being. Countless people have told me that the reason they chose their place of worship was not necessarily for the preaching, but because the church members seemed to genuinely care for one another.

We can't be a caring church without paying attention to what is happening around us. Philippians 2:3–4 reads, "Do nothing from selfishness or empty conceit, but with humility of mind regard one another as more important than yourselves; do not merely look out for your own personal interests, but also for the interests of others."

Sue is a dedicated church leader who always participates in our church's annual gathering for a week of fasting, prayer, and fellowship. One year, on the fourth night of fasting, Sue and her colleagues decided to walk across the church campus to get some information they needed. The walk was far, and when they arrived at their destination, Sue felt particularly weak. Despite her sluggishness, she attempted to give her full attention to the matters being discussed.

The week concluded with a prayer circle, at the end of which several church members approached Sue. After interacting with the first two people, she was a little weak, but as the third person reached her, she felt hot and her chest tightened. Sue finally confessed that she wasn't feeling well. To her surprise, the woman she was speaking to continued making her point as if she hadn't heard a word Sue had said.

Perhaps she didn't hear me, Sue thought, so she spoke up again. But the woman kept talking. Sue clutched her chest, perspiring, struggling to remain conscious. She made her comment a third time. But her colleague continued on to her next topic of conversation.

Sue headed toward a chair but was cut off by another individual who wanted to introduce one of his family members to Sue. She politely waved to the man's mother and again mentioned that she was not feeling well. The man left abruptly.

Finally, a couple who had been standing nearby walked over to offer Sue assistance. They located a physician, who contacted the paramedics.

Sue was interacting with people "up close and personal," but few of them really paid attention to her welfare. They were only concerned about themselves.

On April 20, 1999, Columbine High School experienced a horrific incident—the mass murder of students and a teacher by two students who had been overlooked and taunted by their classmates.

Parents, school administrators, teachers, and students need to pay attention to the people with whom they work or live.

On September 11, 2001, thousands of innocent people were killed in and near the Twin Towers in New York City, at the Pentagon in Washington, DC, and on the United Airlines flight that crashed in Pennsylvania. All members of city, county, state, and federal government bodies need to pay attention to any citizens who might intend us harm.

Andrea Yates drowned her five children. Allegedly, physicians and family members suspected this woman was a potential danger. All family members, neighbors, counselors, and doctors need to pay attention to their spouses, children, neighbors, clients, and patients.

I commonly see unattached women giving church leaders an unhealthy amount of attention. A woman may need assistance, guidance, encouragement, or input from a spiritually strong leader. But if she does not have a strong male presence in her life, the situation is a powder keg sitting next to a lit match. Leaders often do not pay attention to their own vulnerabilities and, as a result, behave improperly with female members of their congregations.

Pastors need to separate themselves from any situation or person that may cause them to stumble. The consequences of not doing so can destroy families. All reverends, elders, deacons, pastors, and church members need to pay attention to situations that could become temptations to sin.

Some marriage partners are in pain. People are struggling with addictions, guilt, financial difficulties, unforgiving attitudes, depression, sexual abuse, anger, and many other painful issues. Many of them are right there in your church pew. Pastors must look for signs, detect pain, and offer divine solutions. God has entrusted us with His flock. We need to take that job seriously.

First Corinthians 12:25 says, "Members may have the same care for one another."

John 13:34 says, "A new commandment I give to you, that you love one another."

1 John 3:11 says, "For this is the message which you have heard

from the beginning, that we should love one another."

John 15:12 states, "This is My commandment, that you love one another, just as I have loved you."

A FINAL NOTE

Pastors, be in tune with your members. Be available to them. And always be real with them.

There is much hidden pain in the pews of our churches today. We pastors must help our parishioners to see that Christ can deliver them from whatever pain they are dealing with.

SUGGESTED RESOURCES

Allender, Dan B. *The Wounded Heart: Hope for Adult Victims of Childhood Sexual Abuse.* Colorado Springs: NavPress, 1990.

Christenson, Larry. *The Christian Family.* Minneapolis: Bethany House Publishers, 1983.

Cloud, Henry. *When Your World Makes No Sense.* Nashville: Thomas Nelson, 1990.

Crabb, Dr. Larry. *The Marriage Builder.* Grand Rapids: Zondervan, 1982.

Flanders, Bill and Marianne. *God's Family Plan.* Kalamazoo: Master's Press, 1976.

Lutzer, Erwin. *Managing Your Emotions.* Wheaton, Ill.: Victor, 1983.

McGee, Robert S. *The Search for Significance.* Nashville: Thomas Nelson, 1998.

Meier, Paul D., Frank B. Minirth, Frank B. Wichern, and Donald Ratcliff. *Introduction to Psychology and Counseling: Christian Perspectives and Applications.* Grand Rapids: Baker, 1991.

Minirth, Frank B. and Paul D. Meier. *Happiness Is a Choice: The Symptoms, Causes, and Cures of Depression.* Grand Rapids: Baker, 1994.

Narramore, Clyde M. *The Psychology of Counseling.* Grand Rapids: Zondervan, 2000.

Seamands, David A. and Gary R. Collins. *Healing for Damaged Emotions.* Wheaton, Ill.: Victor, 1991.

Shuler, Clarence. *Your Wife Can Be Your Best Friend: A Practical Guide for Husbands.* Chicago: Moody, 2000.

Smedes, Lewis B. *Forgive and Forget: Healing the Hurts We Don't Deserve.* New York: Harper San Francisco, 1996.

Swindoll, Chuck. *For Those Who Hurt.* Portland, Ore.: Multnomah, 1977.

Wright, H. Norman. *Communication: Key to Your Marriage: A Practical Guide to Creating a Happy, Fulfilling Relationship.* Ventura: Regal, 2000.

Walvoord, John E. *Christian Counseling for Contemporary Problems.* Dallas: Dallas Theological Seminary, Christian Education Department, 1968.

NOTES

CHAPTER 1: IF YOU ONLY KNEW . . . MY GUILT

1. *The American Heritage® Dictionary of the English Language,* 4th ed., s. v. "guilt."

2. John MacArthur Jr., *The Vanishing Conscience: Drawing the Line in a No-Fault, Guilt-Free World* (Dallas:W Publishing Group, 1995), 36.

3. Robert S. McGee, *The Search for Significance* (Nashville: Thomas Nelson, 1998), 142.

4. Robert Jeffress, *Guilt-Free Living* (Wheaton, Ill:Tyndale House, 1996), 24.

CHAPTER 3: IF YOU ONLY KNEW . . . MY MARITAL CONFLICTS

1. "Divorce Rates: Michigan and United States Occurrences, 1900–2000," Michigan Department of Community Health, available from World Wide Web: www.mdch. state.mi.us/PHA/OSR/marriage/g305.asp?MType=2

2. Rose M.Kreider and Jason M. Fields, *Number, Timing, and Duration of Marriages and Divorces: 1996,* available from World Wide Web: www.census.gov/prod/2002pubs/ p70-80.pdf

CHAPTER 4: IF YOU ONLY KNEW . . . MY FINANCIAL DIFFICULTIES

1. Larry Burkett, *Debt-Free Living: How to Get Out of Debt (And Stay Out)* (Chicago: Northfield, 2001), 16.

CHAPTER 5: IF YOU ONLY KNEW . . . MY SEXUAL PAIN

1. Amy Naugle, Child Sexual Abuse Fact Sheet, "How Common Is Childhood Sexual Abuse?" National Violence Against Women Prevention Research, citing D. G. Kilpatrick, & B. E Saunders (April 1997). "The prevalence of consequences of child victimization," National Institute of Justice Research Preview, U.S. Department of Justice, available from World Wide Web: www.vawprevention.org

CHAPTER 6: IF YOU ONLY KNEW . . . MY ADDICTION

1. *Webster's II New College Dictionary*, s. v. "addict."

2. Anderson M. D. Spickard and Barbara R. Thompson, *Dying for a Drink* (Waco, Tex.: Word, 1996).

CHAPTER 8: THERE IS HOPE

1. *Webster's II New College Dictionary*, s. v. "hope."

If You Only Knew Team

Acquiring Editor:
Greg Thornton

Copy Editor:
Kathy Ide

Back Cover Copy:
Julie-Allyson-Ieron, Joy Media

Cover Design:
Paetzold Associates

Interior Design:
Ragont Design

Printing and Binding:
Versa Press Incorporated

The typeface for the text of this book is
Berkeley